TEAM 6 Together
Activity Book

Contents

Pearson

Starter Let's get started!

1 **Read and complete the sentences.**

> articles   ideas   everyone   find out   ~~new~~   reading   Team

WOW! Blog

1 There are four ____new____ people on the WOW! Team this year. It's going to be a fun year for all of us WOW! _____ members.

2 _____ on the WOW! Team is in Year 6 at school. This is going to be our final year of school. I think that's exciting!

3 The magazine is going to have lots of interesting _____ for people to read. Tell us what you want to _____ about and we'll make the magazine for you!

4 What topics do you like _____ about? Send us some _____. We'd love to hear from you!

2 **Read the ideas on Pupil's Book page 5 again. Then write the names.**

1 Who has read a good book recently? _Riya_

2 Who would like to read about big cities? _____

3 Who enjoys going shopping? _____

4 Who was on an island this summer? _____

5 Who would like to invent things? _____

6 Who likes playing a musical instrument? _____

7 Who wants to read about the future?

8 Who enjoys chatting to friends? _____

9 Who would like to read an adventure story? _____

3 **How interesting are these topics for you? Number them from 1 (the most interesting) to 9 (the least interesting).**

1 Life in the city ☐

2 Jobs in the future ☐

3 Mystery stories ☐

4 Extreme weather ☐

5 Outdoor sports ☐

6 Online communication ☐

7 Shopping centres ☐

8 Great inventions ☐

9 Big celebrations ☐

1 Read the text on Pupil's Book page 6 again and circle *T* (true) or *F* (false). Then explain your answers.

1 Sophia always goes to Argentina in the summer.   **T** / **F**

She often goes to Argentina in the summer.

2 Sophia likes reading books, so she enjoys her English lessons. **T** / **F**

_____

3 Alex enjoys playing team sports and football is his favourite. **T** / **F**

_____

4 Alex says that he doesn't like doing winter sports.   **T** / **F**

_____

5 Mateo is living in England now, close to the sea.   **T** / **F**

_____

6 Mateo has met some friendly people at his new school.   **T** / **F**

_____

7 Mei was born in the UK after her parents came from China.   **T** / **F**

_____

2 Answer the questions about the WOW! Team members. Give reasons.

1 Which person is probably the most athletic?

Alex is probably the most athletic because he talks a lot about sports and outdoor activities.

2 Who probably likes fashion and making things?

_____

3 Which person wants to protect nature and the Earth?

_____

4 Which two people probably speak Spanish at home?

_____

3 💬 Read and complete the questions and write your answers. Then ask and answer with your partner. Write their answers in your notebook.

1 Where _____*do you*_____ come from?   _____

2 How _____ are you?   _____

3 _____ is your birthday?   _____

4 _____ brothers and sisters do you have?   _____

5 _____ your favourite sport?   _____

6 _____ you like this sport so much?   _____

City life

Vocabulary

1 **Unscramble the words to complete the definitions.**

1 A ___*monument*___ (memonunt) is something we build to remember historic events or peopl

2 _____ (gugagel) is a collection of bags that people take with them when they trave

3 A _____ (licepo staiont) is a place where you can talk to a police officer if you have a problem.

4 A _____ (rotu deigu) is a person who shows groups of visitors around a city or other place.

5 A _____ (ttuase) is a large model of a person or animal that is often made of stone

6 _____ (mocoactidano) is any type of place where tourists can stay.

2 **Read the travel forum. Then read and complete the comments.**

1 **Sam**
Last year I visited Rome with my class. It's the ___*capital city*___ of Italy and it's beautiful. Here's a photo of the famous Trevi _____. I threw some coins in it for good luck!

2 **Kyra**
My parents and I visited Canada last year. It has lots of monuments for _____ to visit. Here's a photo of the parliament buildings. There's a big _____ in the centre.

3 **Zac**
I'm a _____, so I don't carry many things, like guide books. When I arrive in a new place, I go to the _____ to ask about fun things to do.

3 **Read the *I'm learning* box. Then complete the lists with words you know.**

> **I'm learning**
>
> **Associating words**
> We can associate new words with other words that we know. This helps us learn and remember the new words.

1 accommodation: *hotel, tent, apartment building*

2 capital city: _____

3 tourist: _____

4 luggage: _____

5 tourist information centre: _____

4 **Write five or more sentences about the capital city of your country.**

1 Read and complete the sentences from the dialogue on Pupil's Book page 10. Who said them? Write. Then listen and check.

> brilliant   burned   do   know   think   ~~visited~~

1 ___Sophia___ I saw in your blog that you ___visited___ The Monument in London.

2 _____ The fire _____ for four days.

3 _____ What did you _____?

4 _____ I didn't _____ that.

5 _____ I thought it was _____.

6 _____ So what did people use to _____ when there was a fire?

2 Read the dialogue again. Circle *T* (true) or *F* (false). Then explain your answers.

1 Sophia wrote a blog about The Monument. **T / F⃝**

_Mateo wrote the blog._____

2 Mateo really enjoyed visiting The Monument. **T / F**

_____

3 Sophia had never heard about The Monument before. **T / F**

_____

4 Nobody knows how the fire of London started. **T / F**

_____

5 There was a fire brigade, but they were too slow. **T / F**

_____

3 Read and complete the dialogues with the correct expressions. Then listen and check.

> (That's amazing!) × 2   (What's up?) × 2   (Oh no! That's awful!) × 2

1 A: You look sad. _____What's up?_____
   B: I didn't do well in my Maths test.

2 A: My family won a trip to Dubai!
   B: _____ You're so lucky!

3 A: It rained every day when I was in Ireland.
   B: _____ Poor you!

4 A: I got all the answers right in the test!
   B: _____ Good for you!

5 A: We had to cancel our beach holiday.
   B: _____ What happened?

6 A: You look busy. _____
   B: Hi Julie. Not much. I'm studying.

4 Work in pairs. Write another dialogue for each expression. Then act out the dialogues.

Grammar

used to

1 🎧 **Listen to Kim and her dad. Read and circle *T* (true) or *F* (false).**

1 Kim's dad didn't use to like History at school. **T / (F)**

2 Kim didn't use to like History, but she likes it now. **T / F**

3 Kim's dad didn't use to have to study hard at Maths. **T / F**

4 Kim's dad used to do really well in his Art exams. **T / F**

5 Kim's dad's favourite hobby used to be playing with computers. **T / F**

6 Kim's favourite school subject is ICT. **T / F**

2 **Read and circle the correct answers.**

1 There **used to** / **didn't use to** be a bakery in Pudding Lane.

2 In 1666, most houses **used to** / **didn't use to** be made of stone.

3 Fires **used to** / **didn't use to** be able to move very quickly.

4 People **used to** / **didn't use to** call the fire brigade.

5 People **used to** / **didn't use to** throw buckets of water over the fire.

3 **Read and complete the sentences with the correct form of *used to*.**

1 I ___didn't use to go___ (go) camping, but now I go four or five times a year. I love it!

2 Many tourists _____ (visit) our town, but now they prefer other places.

3 My dad _____ (be) a tour guide. Now he has his own tour company.

4 People in medieval cities _____ (have) running water at home.

5 I _____ (like) reading poems, but now I'd rather read comics.

4 **Write survey questions. Then write true answers for you.**

When you were younger ...

1 you / be / afraid of the dark?

2 your parents / read to you?

3 your family / go camping?

4 you / watch / cartoons?

5 your friends / play with toys?

6 you / sleep / with the light on?

1 *Did you use to be afraid of the dark?*
No / Yes, I …
_____

2 _____
_____

3 _____
_____

4 _____
_____

5 _____
_____

6 _____
_____

5 💬 **Work with your partner. Ask them your questions from Activity 4 and write their answers in your notebook.**

▶▶ Grammar reference, page 118

1 **After you read** **Read the picture story on Pupil's Book page 12 again. Number the places or things in the city in the order they appear.**

☐ library   ☐ crossroads   ☐ railway station

☐ post office   ☐ bank   ☐ bus station

1 city square   ☐ traffic lights   ☐ roundabout

2 **Answer the questions. Write complete sentences.**

1 What time does the treasure hunt start?

The treasure hunt starts at 10 am.

2 How do the people travel to the city?

_____

3 How does Mum get the first clue?

_____

4 Where do they find the second clue?

_____

5 Where do they find the third clue?

_____

6 Where do the children find the treasure?

_____

3 **Read the *Work with words* box. Read and complete the sentences with compound nouns from the picture story. What other compound nouns can you find in the story? Write.**

> **Work with words**
>
> **Compound nouns**
>
> Compound nouns are formed by two or more words. Sometimes they form one new word and sometimes they stay separate.
>
> *(air + port)* → **airport**
>
> *(tour + guide)* → **tour guide**

1 Cars must always stop when t*raffic lights* are red.

2 There's a c_____ where Park Road meets River Road.

3 Listen! Is that a f_____ e_____? There must be a fire somewhere.

4 Drivers should always slow down when they come to a r_____.

5 Can you give me a ride to the r_____ s_____ please? My train leaves in half an hour.

Other compound nouns: _____

_____

4 **Make compound nouns with a word from each box. Then write five sentences using a compound noun from this lesson.**

1 *In the afternoon ...* _____

2 _____

3 _____

4 _____

5 _____

> ~~after~~ back bath clock foot motor police shopping under

> ball bike centre ground ~~noon~~ pack room station tower

Vocabulary and Grammar

1 🎧 (1.12) **Complete the words. Then listen and tick (✓) the places or things in the city you hear.**

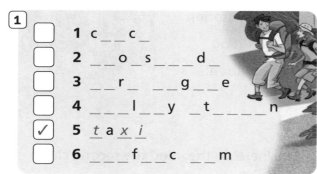

1
- ☐ **1** c _ _ c _
- ☐ **2** _ _ o _ s _ _ _ d _
- ☐ **3** _ _ r _ _ _ g _ _ e
- ☐ **4** _ _ _ l _ _ y _ t _ _ _ _ _ n
- ✓ **5** t a x i
- ☐ **6** _ _ _ _ f _ _ c _ _ _ m

2
- ☐ **7** _ o _ r y
- ☐ **8** _ _ i _ _ b _ _ _ _ h _ _ _ _
- ☐ **9** _ _ v _ m _ _ _ _
- ☐ **10** r _ _ _ _ _ i _ n
- ☐ **11** _ _ u _ _ _ b _ _ _ _
- ☐ **12** _ r _ f _ _ _ _ _ _ g _ _ s

2 **Read and match the definitions to the pictures. Then write the words.**

- **d** | **1** A _train station_ is a place where people go on a train.
- ☐ **2** A _____ is a place where two streets meet and cross each other.
- ☐ **3** A _____ takes you to places around the city but it isn't cheap.
- ☐ **4** A _____ takes things to shops, restaurants and businesses.
- ☐ **5** A _____ is a long queue of cars that isn't moving very quickly.
- ☐ **6** A _____ is the area next to a street where people can walk.

Present continuous and Present simple for future

3 **Read and complete with the Present simple or Present continuous for futur**

> I ¹_am visiting_ my aunt this weekend.
> My parents and I ² _____ (stay)
> at a hotel near my aunt's flat. We
> ³ _____ (not/travel) by car.
> My mum prefers the train.
> It ⁴ _____ (leave) at 7 am
> on Saturday so we
> ⁵ _____ (get up) really early.

Kim   **Paul**

> On Sunday, I ⁶ _____ (have) lunch
> with friends. We ⁷ _____ (meet)
> at a café in our neighbourhood. The café
> ⁸ _____ (open) at 11 am on
> Sundays. After lunch, we
> ⁹ _____ (go) to the cinema. The
> film ¹⁰ _____ (start) at 3 pm so
> we'll have lots of time to talk before that!

4 💡 **Write about your plans for the weekend. Use ideas from the box or your own ideas.**

> go shopping   go to a concert
> have lunch/dinner   meet friends
> see a film/play   play sports
> watch a football match
> go for a walk   visit your grandparents

This weekend ... _____

_____

_____

_____

>> Grammar reference, page 118

1 **After you read** Read the text on Pupil's Book page 14 again. Answer the questions. Use complete sentences.

1 What is the name of Japan's largest island?

The name of Japan's largest island is Honshu.

2 How low can the temperature in Nuuk be in the winter?

3 What is special about Tokyo's Sky Tree tower?

4 Where can people buy fresh fish in Nuuk?

5 How many people pass through the Shinjuku Station in a year?

6 When can visitors see whales near Nuuk?

2 Read the comments from a travel blog. Should the people visit Tokyo, Nuuk or both? Write and explain your answers.

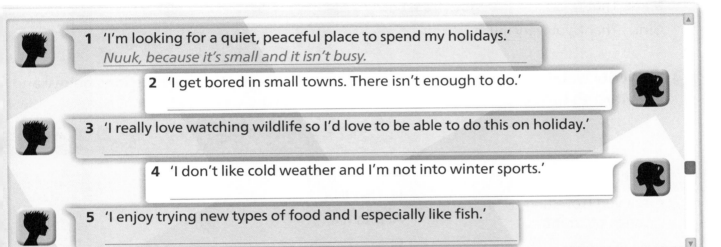

1 'I'm looking for a quiet, peaceful place to spend my holidays.'
Nuuk, because it's small and it isn't busy.

2 'I get bored in small towns. There isn't enough to do.'

3 'I really love watching wildlife so I'd love to be able to do this on holiday.'

4 'I don't like cold weather and I'm not into winter sports.'

5 'I enjoy trying new types of food and I especially like fish.'

3 (1.14) Listen to a report about another capital city. Complete the notes.

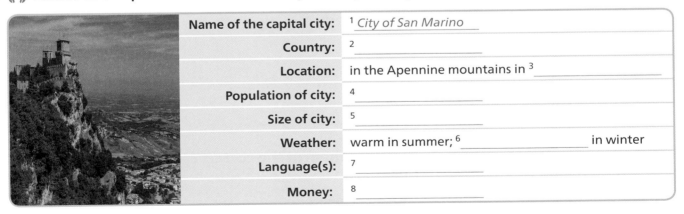

Name of the capital city:	¹ City of San Marino
Country:	²
Location:	in the Apennine mountains in ³
Population of city:	⁴
Size of city:	⁵
Weather:	warm in summer; ⁶ _____ in winter
Language(s):	⁷
Money:	⁸

4 Work in groups. Choose a town or city in your country that would be interesting for tourists and find answers to the questions. Then make a fact file about your town or city.

1 How big is the city?
2 What's its population?
3 What's the language?
4 What money is used?
5 When is a nice time to visit?
6 What can tourists see and do?

1 🎧 (1.17) **Read and complete the dialogue. Then listen and check.**

> 12.45   £57   coach   direct   leave   next   ~~single~~   stop

Girl: Excuse me. How much is a ¹ ___single___ ticket to Bristol?

Man: That'll be ² _____ .

Girl: Is that a ³ _____ coach?

Man: Yes, it is.

Girl: Is the ⁴ _____ coach leaving soon?

Man: Yes, it leaves at ⁵ _____ .

Girl: OK, great. Which bus stop does it ⁶ _____ from?

Man: That ⁷ _____ goes from bus ⁸ _____ 5.

Girl: Thank you very much.

2 ✳ **Write a dialogue between you and a travel assistant. Use the questions below and Activity 1 to help you. Then act out with your partner.**

- Where are you going?
- Are you travelling by coach or train?
- Do you want a single or return ticket?
- Do you need to travel direct?

A: Excuse me. _How much ..._ _____

B: That'll be _____

A: Is that a _____

B: _____

A: _____

B: Yes, _____

A: OK, great. _____

B: That _____

A: _____

Pronunciation

3 🎧 (1.18) 💬 **Listen to the questions. Write them in the correct column. Then practise with your partner.**

The voice goes up ↗	The voice goes down ↘
	How much is a single ticket to Bristol?

Literacy: articles

Reading

Words in context

1 **Read the definitions and write the words. Then match to the pictures.**

century   ground   ~~railway line~~   success   teenager

e	**1** the metal track where a train travels	_railway line_
	2 a hundred years	
	3 a person between 13 and 19 years old	
	4 the surface of the Earth where we walk	
	5 a good end to something that was planned	

2 **Read the article on Pupil's Book page 16 again. Then write the answers.**

1 People who live in cities think these are very important.   _green spaces_

2 This used to run over the streets of Manhattan.

3 This is a a beautiful place high above Manhattan.

4 These people like to visit the High Line park.

5 This space used to be a station under the ground.

6 This helps get sunlight down to the Lowline park.

3 **Read the sentences and write _T_ (true), _F_ (false) or _DS_ (doesn't say). Then explain your answers.**

1 There are lots of places to make new parks in New York City.

| F | _There aren't lots of places to make new parks in New York City._ |

2 The High Line closed in the 1980s because it was too expensive.

3 Sam Watts likes the High Line because it isn't noisy or dangerous.

4 There are going to be vegetable gardens in the Lowline park.

5 James Ramsey thinks the old Lowline station is too dark.

4 **Work in groups. Imagine you are planning a new park in your area. Discuss the questions and make notes. Then share your ideas with the class.**

1 Where are you going to make a new park?

2 What is in this place now?

3 Are people using this place now? Why?/Why not?

4 Why is it a good place to make a park?

5 What type of park are you going to make?

6 Who is going to enjoy using your park?

Literacy: articles

Writing

> **either ... or**
> We use *either ... or* to talk about a choice between two things. *The best time of year in Edinburgh is **either** the arts festival in August **or** New Year.*

1 <u>Underline</u> the two options. Then write one sentence using *either ... or.*

1 We'd like to <u>visit the castle</u>. We'd like to <u>visit the museum</u>.

We'd like to visit either the castle or the museum.

2 My grandparents travel in summer. They travel in autumn.

_____

3 You can come shopping with me. You can stay at the hotel.

_____

4 They want to have spaghetti. They want to have pizza.

_____

5 She can watch a musical. She can watch a puppet show.

_____

6 Santiago always wears jeans. He always wears shorts.

_____

2 Plan an article about a city you want to visit in the future.

Write an introduction. What city do you want to visit? Where is it? Is it a capital city?

Paragraph 1: What's the most famous place there? What's interesting about this place?

Paragraph 2: What are the best times of year to visit? What month do you want to go there?

Write a conclusion. Are you excited about the trip? Are you going to have a good time? Why?

3 Now write your article.

4 Check your work. Tick (✓) the steps when you have done them.

Have I used present tenses correctly? ☐

Have I used *either ... or* correctly? ☐

Have I included an introduction and a conclusion? ☐

Have I used clear paragraphs? ☐

Have I used formal language? ☐

Have I checked my facts? ☐

1 **Label the pictures.**

<u>_clock tower_</u>

_____

_____

_____

_____

_____

_____

_____

2 **Unscramble the words to complete the sentences.**

1 I left my bag on the _____ _coach_ _____ (ohcac) and someone took it!

2 My aunt lives in a nice _____ (gbodenoihuorh).

3 Go to the next _____ (sracordsos) and turn left.

4 Wow! I just found £5 on the _____ (matepven).

5 They built a _____ (nntomemu) to the first President.

6 It's hard to find _____ (cacimomdotaon) in London.

3 **What were you like when you were a baby? Write true sentences with *used to*.**

1 I play / teddy bears <u>_I used to play with_</u>
<u>_teddy bears._</u>

2 have / mobile phone _____

3 be / noisy _____

4 sleep / a lot _____

5 read / books _____

6 tidy / my room _____

4 **Read and complete the text. Use the Present simple and Present continuous tenses.**

Valentina [1] _is going_ (go) to a concert this evening. It [2] _____ (start) at 7 pm.
She [3] _____ (meet) her friends at the bus station. They [4] _____ (catch) bus 17 to
the concert hall. The bus [5] _____ (leave) the station at 6 pm.

Self-evaluation

5 **Answer the questions about your work in Unit 1.**

1 How was your work in this unit? Choose. ☐ OK ☐ Good ☐ Excellent

2 Which lesson was your favourite? _____

3 Which parts of the unit were difficult for you? _____

4 What new things can you talk about now? _____

5 How can you work and learn better in the next unit? _____

Get ready for...

A2 Key for Schools Listening Part 2

Think! ① Read the task carefully. Make sure you know what you have to do.

Try! ② 🎧 1.21 Listen. For each question, choose the correct answer. Then explain your answers.

1 Where is the boy's class going to go first today?

A a police station **B** a museum **C** a restaurant

_____

2 About how many students are going on the trip?

A twenty-five **B** fifty **C** a hundred

_____

3 When will the boy arrive at home this evening?

A 4 pm **B** 5 pm **C** 3 pm

_____

Do! ③ 🎯 🎧 1.22 For each question, write the correct answer in each gap. You will hear a father talking to his daughter about a school trip. Write one word or a number or a date or a time.

School Trip to London

The coach leaves: at _____8.30 am_____

1 What they'll see at Trafalgar Square: monuments and _____

2 The building they'll visit in the morning: The National _____

3 What they'll eat in Covent Garden:

_____

4 How long they'll be at the Palace of Westminster:

_____ hours

5 Where the coach will pick them up: near Victoria _____

tip Exam

Listen to each recording for the first time to find the specific information and copy it into the gap. When you listen to the recording for the second time, check your answers.

A2 Key for Schools Reading and Writing Part 2

 1 Read the task carefully. Make sure you know what you have to do.

 2 Read the texts and the questions. Write the correct names.

> Last summer, I visited London with my parents. We spent every day visiting monuments and museums, so we were always tired in the evening. My favourite place was the Tower of London.

George

> I went to London last week, but it was only for a school trip. We visited the British Museum in the morning and then went shopping in the afternoon. I might go back again next month to see a concert.

Holly

Which person ...

1 spent less time in London?   _Holly_

2 visited more than one museum?   _____

3 didn't travel with family?   _____

 3 🎯 For each question, choose the correct answer.

tip Exam

Begin by carefully reading the three descriptions of the people. Next, read the questions and underline any matches between these and the descriptions.

Which person ...	Sarah	Robert	Emma	
1 is staying with family?	A	B	C	_C_
2 will explore a capital city?	A	B	C	___
3 may need to take a tent?	A	B	C	___
4 prefers quiet holidays?	A	B	C	___
5 will travel in the autumn?	A	B	C	___

 Sarah: Next summer, I'm going to Edinburgh on holiday. It's the capital city of Scotland. It has lots of beautiful monuments and other things to see. We won't need a tour guide because my Aunt Betty lives there. We've found a nice hotel in the city centre to stay in.

Robert: I'm visiting Scotland next October with my friends. We're going camping in the Highlands, so we won't be visiting Edinburgh this time. I'm not taking much because it all has to fit in my backpack! I hope it doesn't rain when we're there. I hate it when my sleeping bag gets wet!

 **Emma:** This year I'm spending August with my grandparents in Dunbar, in Scotland. It's a town on the coast, not far from Edinburgh. Some people like busy cities, but I prefer calm places where you can relax, walk on the beach, or go camping if you like. I think it's more relaxing.

2 Our future

Vocabulary

1 **Read and complete the sentences.**

1 A ___novelist___ writes stories for children or adults.

2 An _____ makes new inventions.

3 A _____ works in and under the water.

4 A _____ looks after people's teeth.

5 A _____ cuts people's hair.

6 A _____ interviews people and then writes articles for a newspaper.

2 **Read the comments. What job would be good for each person? Write.**

1 I like leading other people and organising things.

___manager___

2 I'm really good at football. I practise every day.
_____

3 I like drawing new houses and other buildings.
_____

4 I enjoy making new games for my tablet and my phone.
_____

5 I'm good at making posters and adverts on a computer.
_____

6 I want to do things to make my city and my country better.
_____

3 **Read the _I'm learning_ box. Then complete the jobs with the correct suffixes.**

I'm learning

Suffixes for jobs
Many jobs in English have suffixes, such as -er, -or, -ist and –ian.
di**ver**   novel**ist**
camera oper**ator**   politic**ian**

1 sing**er** _____
2 art_____
3 music_____
4 build_____
5 doct_____
6 librar_____
7 scient_____
8 act_____

4 **Write five or more sentences about jobs you know. What do the people do? Where do they work? Which jobs seem interesting to you?**

1 (2.4) **Read and complete the sentences from the dialogue on Pupil's Book page 22. Then listen and check.**

1 I think you'll be a ___brilliant___ footballer for one of the _____ teams!

2 Ah, that's _____ of you to say, but I _____ think that will happen.

3 I'll _____ practising and who _____ what will happen.

4 You do _____ a great job designing and _____ the WOW! website.

5 No, I _____. I've always _____ to be an architect.

6 What _____ of house will you want to _____ in?

2 **Read the dialogue again. Circle T (true) or F (false). Then explain your answers.**

1 Mei thinks Alex will be a good footballer. (T)/ F *She thinks he'll be brilliant.* _____

2 Alex thinks he'll join an important team. T / F _____

3 Alex says he's going to stop practising. T / F _____

4 Alex thinks Mei is great with computers. T / F _____

5 Mei has designed a new house for Alex. T / F _____

6 Alex knows exactly what house he wants. T / F _____

3 (2.5) **Read and complete the dialogues with the correct expressions. Then listen and check.**

| Oh cool! | × 2 | I disagree! | × 2 | I'm not sure. | × 2 |

1 A: I'm selling my old bike. Do you want it?
   B: *I'm not sure.* Can I think about it?

2 A: Computer programmers have easy jobs.
   B: _____ They have to work really hard!

3 A: I'm having a party next Friday.
   B: _____ I love parties!

4 A: This new cartoon on TV is terrible.
   B: _____ I think it's great!

5 A: Is life better in small towns or big cities?
   B: _____ Both have good points.

6 A: I want to study hairdressing.
   B: _____ You can cut my hair!

4 **Work in pairs. Write another dialogue for each expression. Then act out the dialogues.**

Grammar

will for predictions

1 🎧 (2.8) **Listen and complete the sentences with *will* or *won't*.**

 Mario

 Kate

1 Mario ___will___ become a language teacher.

2 He _____ learn Italian next year.

3 He _____ live somewhere in Europe.

4 Kate _____ be a professional athlete.

5 She _____ go to university one day.

6 She _____ need to study photography.

2 **Read and complete the sentences with *will* or *won't* and the verbs in the box.**

> buy   eat   go   ~~rain~~   study   watch

1 You don't need to bring that umbrella. It ___won't rain___ this afternoon.

2 After she finishes studying, Sudarat _____ TV for an hour or two. She needs to relax.

3 My friends and I _____ cycling on Saturday if the weather is nice and sunny.

4 Ali probably _____ very much for dinner because he had a big lunch today.

5 My parents _____ me a new tablet if I don't pass all my exams.

6 I _____ computer programming at university because I want to design apps and games.

3 💡 **Order the words to make questions with *will*. Then write true answers for y**

1 day   you   teacher   will   a   become   one   ?
Will you become a teacher one day?

2 work   a   for   company   you   will   big   ?
_____

3 another   your   will   country   live   family   in   ?
_____

4 learn   any   you   languages   will   foreign   ?
_____

5 town   home   will   a   be   your   in   small   ?
_____

6 lot   you   a   will   children   have   of   ?
_____

4 **Write questions about the future with *will*. Use the ideas in the box or your own ideas.**

> where / live?   what / study?
> when / start working?   what job / have?
> where / travel?   when / have children?

1 *Where will you live?*
2 _____
3 _____
4 _____
5 _____
6 _____

5 💬 **Work with your partner. Ask them the questions from Activity 4 and write their answers in your notebook.**

>> Grammar reference, page 119

1 **After you read** Read the poem on Pupil's Book page 24 again. Then read and complete the sentences.

1 Lisa says she was born on _____Tuesday_____ 29th May.

2 She says she may go _____ around the world.

3 Lisa might go to _____ and study English or Maths.

4 She could become either a _____ or an astronaut.

5 Lisa may fall in _____ and she may get married.

6 She could live somewhere in the city or in the _____ .

2 Answer the questions. Use complete sentences.

1 When might Lisa go backpacking?

She might go backpacking when she leaves school.

2 When will Lisa get a job?

_____

3 Will Lisa fall in love one day?

_____

4 Where might Lisa live in the city?

_____

5 How many children will Lisa have?

_____

6 When will Lisa look back at her life?

_____

3 Read the *Work with words* box. Write the homophones for these words.

Work with words

Homophones

Homophones are words that sound the same but have different meanings. Sometimes they have different spellings, too.

*We'll have to wait and **see**.* *I might sit by the **sea**.*

*I was born in **May**.* *I **may** go out later.*

1 too	*two*	7 for	_____
2 son	_____	8 their	_____
3 won	_____	9 hear	_____
4 meat	_____	10 right	_____
5 know	_____	11 wear	_____
6 bye	_____	12 hour	_____

4 Write five sentences with pairs of homophones.   *I have two cats, too.*

Vocabulary and Grammar

1 Complete the life events. Then tick
(✓) the five most important life
events for you.

> get ~~be~~ go have fall find get
> go grow go retire move

It's your life!

✓	1	_be_	born
☐	2	_____	up
☐	3	_____	to school
☐	4	_____	backpacking
☐	5	_____	to university
☐	6	_____	a degree
☐	7	_____	a job
☐	8	_____	in love
☐	9	_____	married
☐	10	_____	house
☐	11	_____	children
☐	12	_____	

2 (2.12) Listen to Paul and his grandma.
Then listen again and write the life
events you hear.

1	_be born_	5	_____
2	_____	6	_____
3	_____	7	_____
4	_____	8	_____

might, *may* and *could* for predictions

3 Look at the table. Then write sentences
with *will*, *won't*, *may (not)*, *might (not)*
or *could*.

Life events	Maksim	Me
1 go to university one day	*Yes! For sure!*	*I'm not sure.*
2 move to a town in the UK	*I don't think so.*	
3 get married before age 30	*Maybe. I hope so!*	
4 become a Maths teacher	*No way! Never!*	
5 have two children	*I don't think so.*	
6 retire before age 65	*Yes! Definitely!*	

1 _Maksim will go to university one day._

2 _____

3 _____

4 _____

5 _____

6 _____

4 💡 Write your answers in the table
in Activity 3. Then write sentences
with *will*, *won't*, *may (not)*, *might
(not)* or *could*.

1 _I might go to university one day._

2 _____

3 _____

4 _____

5 _____

6 _____

>>> Grammar reference, page 119

 **Culture** ②

1 [After you read] **Read the text on Pupil's Book page 26 again. What do the sentences describe?**

1 It's a name for a man who is getting married.   *the groom* _____

2 It takes place at the end of the school year.   _____

3 These objects are made of gold or wood.   _____

4 They are a boy and a girl that the school chooses.   _____

5 It's a tradition that comes from ancient times.   _____

6 Indian women have them on their hands and feet.   _____

2 **Answer the questions. Write complete sentences.**

1 What do Chinese girls wear for their special celebration?
   They wear traditional clothes. _____

2 What decorations do Chinese girls put in their hair?
   _____

3 What do students in the USA wear for their prom?
   _____

4 When do some British children celebrate a prom?
   _____

5 How long do wedding celebrations last in India?
   _____

6 What do Indian brides and grooms wear for weddings?
   _____

3 (2.14) **Listen to a report about another celebration. Complete the text.**

In the Philippines, there is a special celebration which takes place when a ¹____*girl*____ becomes ²_____ years old. This is when girls officially become ³_____ . This celebration is called a debut. The number is very important so the girl will invite eighteen ⁴_____ to a big party. She may also light eighteen ⁵_____ for good luck. She might also receive eighteen ⁶_____ , such as red roses. During the party, the girl dances with her ⁷_____ , grandfather or another man from her family. It's a very special ⁸_____ in Philippine culture.

4 📶 **Work in groups. Choose one of the celebrations in the box and find answers to the questions. Write about your celebration.**

| Sweet Sixteen (USA)   Seijin no Hi (Japan)   Quinceañera (Mexico)   Land diving (Vanuatu) |

1 When does the celebration happen?   3 Who participates in the celebration?

2 Why is the celebration important?   4 What happens during the celebration?

English in action
Making and responding to offers of help

1 (2.17) **Read and complete the dialogue. Then listen and check.**

bring you some   but no need   help you   hand   let me help
need any help   ~~film party~~   this food

Mila: The kitchen is a mess after our ¹____*film party*____ .
I have to tidy it.

Ana: Would you like a ²_____, Mila?
I'll put ³_____ away in the fridge.

Mila: That would be great!

Kim: ⁴_____ you, too. I'll sweep the floor.

Mila: Thanks! I'll do the washing-up.

Ana: I've put away the food. Do you
⁵_____ with the washing-up?

Mila: Thanks, ⁶_____! Now I'll get us
something cool to drink.

Kim: Can I ⁷_____ with that?

Ana: Wait! I'll help you, too!

Mila: No, don't worry! Sit down and I'll
⁸_____ juice!

2 ☀ **Read and complete the dialogues with your own ideas. Then act out the dialogues with your partner.**

1 A: Oh, dear! These boxes are so big!
  B: Do *you need any help with them?*_____
  A: *That would be great!*_____

2 A: I can't understand my Maths homework.
  B: I'll_____
  A: _____

3 A: I have to tidy up the garage today.
  B: Let _____
  A: _____

4 A: I hate cleaning the windows.
  B: I'll _____
  A: _____

5 A: I'm going to make some sandwiches.
  B: Can _____
  A: _____

6 A: I need to load the dishwasher.
  B: Would_____
  A: _____

Pronunciation

3 (2.18) 💬 **Listen and read the sentences. Circle the stressed words. Then practise with your partner.**

1 We ⟨could⟩⟨go⟩ to the ⟨cinema⟩ later.
2 She might make some pizza.
3 I may have a party.

4 They might need some help.
5 He may go to university.
6 You could tidy the kitchen.

Literacy: blogs

Reading

Words in context

1 **Read the definitions and write the words.**

blog   feeling   housework   ~~idea~~   opinion

1 This is something you think about and plan in your mind. _____idea_____

2 This is a personal journal that is written on the internet. _____

3 This is something you sense or feel, usually with your body. _____

4 This is your personal preference or view about something. _____

5 These are jobs we do at home, such as vacuuming the carpet. _____

2 **Read the blog on Pupil's Book page 28 again. Read and complete the sentences with two words.**

1 Samira was having a conversation _____about robots_____ with her friends.

2 She thinks that if robots do all _____, we won't have any work.

3 Samira doesn't think there's _____ to worry about the future.

4 Robots do many jobs that people _____ do in the past.

5 In the future, robots _____ cars and do many other things.

6 Robots won't be able _____ a teacher's or a nurse's job.

3 **Read the sentences and circle _T_ (true) or _F_ (false). Then explain your answers.**

1 Samira thinks robots are going to take all our jobs. **T** /Ⓕ

She doesn't think robots are going
to take all our jobs

2 Samira says that robots already build cars for us. **T / F**

_____

3 Samira thinks robots can do more interesting jobs now. **T / F**

_____

4 Samira says that people will be able to learn about new things. **T / F**

_____

5 Samira thinks robots have could have feelings one day. **T / F**

_____

6 Samira says that robots will never understand teachers. **T / F**

_____

4 **Work in groups. Look at the ideas in the box and decide if robots could do that job in the future. Discuss and make notes. Then share your ideas with the class.**

design computer games   draw beautiful paintings   give people advice
make action films   take care of our pets   write popular songs

Literacy: blogs

Writing

1 **Read and complete the sentences with *because* or *so*. Use a comma where necessary.**

Will we need to study languages in the future?

1 Everyone will speak one language, _____*so*_____ they won't need to study any others.

2 We won't need to study languages _____ computers will translate everything.

3 Countries won't lose their languages _____ people will try to protect them.

4 We'll meet aliens from other worlds _____ we'll have to learn their language.

5 People will study robot languages _____ robots will never understand people.

6 We'll learn languages while we sleep _____ we won't need to take classes.

tip **Writing**

so and *because*
We use *so* to link two ideas when the second idea is the result of the first idea. We use a comma before *so*. We use *because* to link two ideas when the second idea is a reason for the first idea. We don't use a comma with *because*.

2 **Plan a blog called *Will we need to study languages in the future?***

Paragraph 1: Explain the topic of your blog. →

Paragraph 2: Explain your opinions about the topic. Use phrases: *In my opinion …, In my view …*, etc. Use *so* and *because* to link two ideas. →

Paragraph 3: Write about your final ideas on the topic. Use linking words: *also, in addition, what's more*, etc. →

3 **Now write your blog.**

4 **Check your work. Tick (✓) the steps when you have done them.**

Have I explained the topic of my blog clearly? ☐

Have I explained my opinions and used *so* and *because* correctly? ☐

Have I used introductory phrases? ☐

Have I used linking works correctly? ☐

1 **Look at the pictures and write the jobs.**

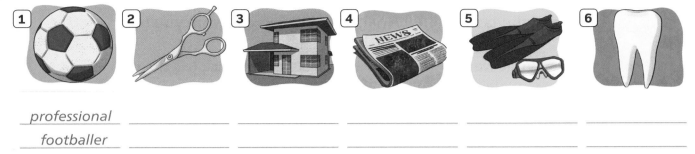

| 1 | 2 | 3 | 4 | 5 | 6 |

professional _____ _____ _____ _____ _____
footballer _____ _____ _____ _____ _____

2 **Read and complete the text.**

MY DAD'S FROM THE USA

He was ¹ _____born_____ in New York City in 1973. His family moved
² _____ when he was a baby and he grew ³ _____ in Miami.
That's where he went to ⁴ _____ until he was eighteen. He then
went to ⁵ _____ and studied to become a doctor. After he got his
⁶ _____, my dad went ⁷ _____ in Europe for six months.
He met my mum in Italy and they fell in ⁸ _____. They got ⁹ _____
in Miami and then they had two ¹⁰ _____, me and my sister!

3 **Write questions about the future with _will_. Then write true answers for you.**

1 | you | / | become | / | an actor?   _Will you become an actor?_   _No, I won't._

2 | you | / | study | / | graphic design?   _____ _____

3 | you | / | go backpacking | / | around the world?   _____ _____

4 | you | / | live | / | near the sea?   _____ _____

5 | you | / | retire | / | you're sixty?   _____ _____

4 **Write predictions about your personal future.**

1 I might _____ after I finish
school.

2 I may not _____ before I'm
eighteen.

3 I could _____ before I get a job.

4 I may _____ after I get married.

5 I might not _____ before I'm
thirty.

Self-evaluation

5 **Answer the questions about your work in Unit 2.**

1 How was your work in this unit? Choose.   ☐ OK   ☐ Good   ☐ Excellent

2 Which lesson was your favourite? _____

3 Which parts of the unit were difficult for you? _____

4 What new things can you talk about now? _____

5 How can you work and learn better in the next unit? _____

Get ready for...

A2 Key for Schools Listening Part 1

 1 Read the task carefully. Make sure you know what you have to do.

 2 (2.21) **What was Grandad's first job? Listen and tick (✓) the correct picture. Then explain your answer.**

A ☐   B ☐   C ☐

Do! **3** (2.22) **Listen. For each question, choose the correct answer.**

> **tip Exam**
>
> Listen to the whole dialogue before you choose your answer. The correct answer may be at the end of the dialogue.

1 What does David want to be when he's older?

A ☐   B ☐   C ☐

3 Where does Sophia want to study next summer?

A ☐   B ☐   C ☐

2 Who is the journalist going to interview?

A ☐   B ☐   C ☐

4 When will they have a meeting with the architect?

A ☐   B ☐   C ☐

A2 Key for Schools Reading and Writing Part 6

 1 Read the task carefully. Make sure you know what you have to do.

 2 Read the email from Katy. Then number the parts of the email.

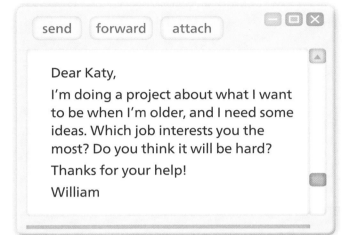

send forward attach

Dear Katy,

I'm doing a project about what I want to be when I'm older, and I need some ideas. Which job interests you the most? Do you think it will be hard?

Thanks for your help!

William

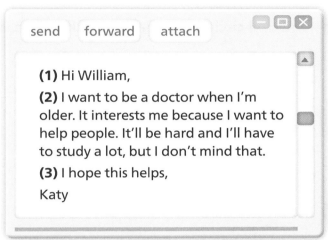

send forward attach

(1) Hi William,

(2) I want to be a doctor when I'm older. It interests me because I want to help people. It'll be hard and I'll have to study a lot, but I don't mind that.

(3) I hope this helps,

Katy

main body ☐   **greeting** 1   **ending** ☐

Do! **3** 🎯 Your English friend, Frank, wants to know about what you want to be when you're older. Write an email to Frank. Write 35 words or more.

tip **Exam**

Make sure you answer all the questions in the main body of your email. Don't forget the greeting and the ending.

In the email:
- tell Frank what you want to be
- say why you think this job is interesting
- say if you think it will be hard or not

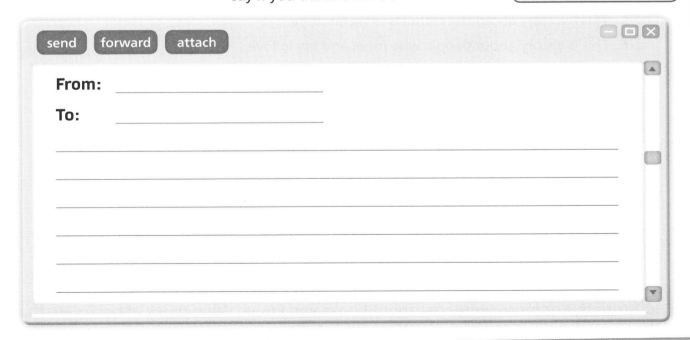

send forward attach

From: _____

To: _____

_____
_____
_____
_____
_____
_____

Let's read!

Vocabulary

1 Find and circle the types of books. Then write.

1 d _rama_
2 h_____ story
3 p_____
4 s_____ fiction
5 m_____
6 a_____ story

7 f_____
8 g_____ novel
9 r_____
10 d_____ story
11 b_____
12 r_____ book

S	D	Y	D	E	X	T	Y	R	Z
C	R	S	E	R	G	N	R	E	J
I	A	A	T	U	R	B	T	C	F
E	M	T	E	T	A	H	E	I	E
N	A	N	C	N	P	O	O	P	C
C	V	A	T	E	H	R	P	E	N
E	D	F	I	V	I	R	I	I	A
Q	V	K	V	D	C	O	D	V	M
Q	G	J	E	A	J	R	C	A	O
B	I	O	G	R	A	P	H	Y	R
Z	M	Y	S	T	E	R	Y	K	Q

2 Match the pictures to the descriptions. Then write the book types from Activity 1.

a  b   c  d  e  f

c **1** This is a true story about the life of a famous person.   _biography_

☐ **2** This is a scary story that makes people feel afraid.   _____

☐ **3** This is a book that has lots of pictures and some text.   _____

☐ **4** This a book of instructions for making delicious food.   _____

☐ **5** This is a story about the future and technology.   _____

☐ **6** This is a story about people who meet and fall in love.   _____

3 💡 Read the *I'm learning* box. Then write the adjective form of the nouns.
Use a dictionary to help you.

> ### I'm learning
> **Nouns to adjectives**
> Many nouns have an adjective form.
> We often make these forms by adding
> suffixes, such as *-ic, -ous,* and *-ible.*
> *poetry → poetic   horror → horrible*
> *adventure → adventurous*

1 drama   _dramatic_
2 mystery   _____
3 romance   _____
4 terror   _____
5 fantasy   _____

6 danger   _____
7 science   _____
8 fame   _____
9 energy   _____

4 💡 Write five or more sentences about books you know. What types of books are they?
What are they like? Use the adjectives from Activity 3.

1 (3.4) **Read and complete the sentences from the dialogue on Pupil's Book page 34. Who said them? Write. Then listen and check.**

~~book survey~~   drama   exciting   hold on   recipe books   tell me

1 _Sophia_ Alex told me that you had the results of our ___book survey___ .

2 _____ _____, let me find them on my computer.

3 _____ That doesn't surprise me. They're the most _____.

4 _____ A lot of students said that they didn't like _____.

5 _____ Can you _____ some of the other results?

6 _____ Some students said that they used _____ at home.

2 **Read the dialogue again and circle _T_ (true) or _F_ (false). Then explain your answers.**

1 More than 100 people did the survey. (T)/ F _Over 100 students answered the survey._

2 Some people said that they didn't like reading. T / F _____

3 Detective stories weren't very popular. T / F _____

4 Sophia has a sister who enjoys drama. T / F _____

5 Lots of students said that they liked poetry. T / F _____

6 Sophia suggesting doing an online activity. T / F _____

3 (3.5) **Read and complete the dialogues with the correct expressions. Then listen and check.**

Hold on, × 2   What a shame. × 2   Sure, no problem. × 2

1 A: Can you help me, please? I've lost my phone.

B: ¹_____Hold on,_____ let me turn off the TV and help you.

A: I can't find it anywhere.

B: ²_____ Poor you!

A: Can you call my phone? Maybe someone will answer it.

B: ³_____ What's your number?

2 A: I'm doing really badly in Maths.

B: Really? ⁴_____

A: I need to study more. Can you help me?

B: ⁵_____ We can study together.

A: Are you free on Tuesday after school?

B: ⁶_____ I need to check my diary. Yes, I'm free on Tuesday.

A: Great, thanks.

4 **Work in pairs. Write another dialogue for each expression. Then act out the dialogues.**

Grammar

Reported speech

1 🎧(3.8) **Listen and tick (✓) the correct sentences.**

1 Mark said that …

  a ✓ he loved science fiction books.

  b ☐ he was keen on detective stories.

  c ☐ he didn't collect graphic novels.

2 Tina told her brother that …

  a ☐ she preferred mystery stories.

  b ☐ horror stories were too boring.

  c ☐ Dracula is good.

3 Emma said that …

  a ☐ she always read lots of novels.

  b ☐ she was interested in history.

  c ☐ she wanted to write a biography.

2 **Read and complete the dialogue with reported speech.**

Max — I want to buy a new book. **Ana**

There's a good bookshop on King Street.

They don't sell graphic novels there.

You need to try other types of books.

I don't know what other types to try.

I can give you some suggestions.

1 Max told Ana that *he wanted to buy* a new book.

2 Ana said that _____ a good bookshop on King Street.

3 Max told Ana that _____ graphic novels there.

4 Ana told Max that _____ to try other types of books.

5 Max said that _____ what other types to try.

6 Ana told Max that _____ him some suggestions.

3 **Read and write the sentences as reported speech.**

1 The teacher told me, 'You're late for class.'

The teacher told me that I was late for class.

2 I said, 'Romance novels don't interest me.'

_____

3 Lisa told us, 'You have to read my new poem.'

_____

4 The boys said, 'We want to see a horror film.'

_____

5 I told my friends, 'You need to help me study.'

_____

6 Katy said, 'My brother doesn't read very much.'

_____

4 **Read Katia's answers to the survey. Then rewrite her answers as reported speech.**

1 comment
Alex   1 day ago

Book Survey
1 What books do you enjoy reading?
2 Are there books you don't like reading?
3 Where do you usually read?
4 What's your favourite book?
5 What do you want to read next?

1 comment
Katia   5 minutes ago

5 minutes
I enjoy reading science fiction books and poetry. I don't like mystery or detective stories. I usually read at home in my bedroom. My favourite book is A Wrinkle in Time. I want to read a book called The Wild Robot.

Katia said that she enjoyed reading science fiction and poetry.

_____

_____

_____

》》 Grammar reference, page 120

WOW! Book Club 3

1 **After you read** (3.9) (3.10) **Read and listen to the mystery story on Pupil's Book page 36 again. Number the events in order.**

- [ ] **a** The children went inside and used their torches.
- [ ] **b** People returned and the tower became famous.
- [ ] **c** Nina and Ben went to the tower to see what was happening.
- [ ] **d** They found pictures of animals on the tower.
- [ ] **e** People suddenly stopped visiting the old tower.
- [ ] **f** The cow was very happy when it was free again.
- [1] **g** There was an old tower that many people visited.
- [ ] **h** They solved the mystery and let the animal go free.

2 **Answer the questions. Write complete sentences.**

1 Who used to visit the tower and why did they go there?

Tourists used to visit the tower to see the paintings on the wall.

2 What happened when people heard the strange noise?

_____

3 What pictures did Ben and Nina see on the walls of the tower?

_____

4 What did Nina and Ben find when they turned on their torches?

_____

5 What did Nina think the cow was saying to them?

_____

3 **Read the *Work with words* box. Write the nouns. Use a dictionary to help you.**

Work with words

The noun suffix *-ness*

Some nouns are formed by adding the suffix *-ness* to adjectives. Sometimes there are spelling changes.

fit (adj) → **fitness** *(noun)*

happy (adj) → **happiness** *(noun)*

1 bright _____*brightness*_____

2 dark _____

3 empty _____

4 great _____

5 ill _____

6 kind _____

7 sad _____

8 strange _____

9 tidy _____

4 **Write five sentences using a noun with *-ness* suffix in each sentence.**

Vocabulary and Grammar

1 **Read the clues and complete the crossword.**

1 Something without anything inside is …
2 Something that is very large is …
3 Something without any light is …
4 Something that is very bad is …
5 Something that is very small is …
6 Something that is very beautiful is …
7 Something that has lots of light is …
8 Something that we don't know anything about is …
9 Something that is unusual is …

1 E M P T Y

Present and Past simple passive

2 **Read and circle the correct words.**

1 I love this selfie. It **is / (was) / were** taken by my dad last weekend.

2 My new shoes **aren't / wasn't / isn't** made of leather. They're plastic.

3 The Tower of London **are / is / were** visited by thousands of people every year.

4 I don't know why we **wasn't / isn't / weren't** invited to the party.

5 Those singers **are / is / was** known around the world for their music.

6 Our house **isn't / weren't / wasn't** damaged in the big storm last week.

3 **Write sentences with the Present or Past simple passive.**

Wingham Manor ^{1} _is located_ (locate) in the north of the country. It ^{2}_____ (know) for its large, beautiful gardens. The house and gardens ^{3}_____ (visit) by many tourists every year. The house ^{4}_____ (build) about 200 years ago, but it ^{5}_____ (not/design) to be a home. It ^{6}_____ (make) to be a holiday residence. Some rooms ^{7}_____ (damage) in a fire fifty years ago and nobody has stayed in the house since then. The house and gardens ^{8}_____ (buy) by the town and now they ^{9}_____ (use) for many local celebrations.

4 **Write five passive sentences about a famous building you know. Use the words in the box or your own ideas.**

build   buy   damage   design   know   locate   make   sell   use   visit

Grammar reference, page 120

1 **After you read** Read the text on Pupil's Book page 38 again. Then read and complete the sentences with two words from the box.

book　bright　cities　Greek
language　large　lost　mysterious
Norwegian　strange　valley　writer

1 The Voynich Manuscript is a _____ *mysterious book* _____ .

2 We can't read the manuscript because it's written in a _____ that we don't understand.

3 The Hessdalen Lights appear in the sky above a _____ .

4 The Hessdalen Lights are _____ and _____ .

5 Atlantis is one of the most famous _____ in history.

6 Plato was a _____ who wrote about Atlantis.

2 Answer the questions. Use complete sentences.

1 What pictures can people see in the Voynich Manuscript?

   People can see gorgeous pictures of flowers
   and leaves.

2 What type of book could the Voynich Manuscript be?

   _____

3 What do the Hessdalen Lights do in the sky?

   _____

4 The Hessdalen lights might be as large as what?

   _____

5 Where did Plato think Atlantis might be?

   _____

6 Where do other people think Atlantis might be?

   _____

3 (3.14) Listen to a report about another mystery. Complete the text.

The Nazca Lines are very [1]___*mysterious*___ . They are on the ground in the Nazca [2]_____ in southern Peru. They were made by [3]_____ and some of them are about [4]_____ years old. A professor from the [5]_____ rediscovered the lines in [6]_____ . He was flying over the area when he noticed the [7]_____ lines. He found pictures of plants, [8]_____ and people, too. The pictures haven't [9]_____ away because it almost never [10]_____ in the desert. Some people think the Nazca lines are religious or astronomical symbols. We [11]_____ never know for sure, but we can [12]_____ the beauty of these ancient pictures.

4 📶 Work in groups. Choose one of the mysterious places in the box and find answers to the questions. Write about your mysterious place.

Derinkuyu (Turkey)　Stonehenge (England)　The Pyramids of Giza (Egypt)
Yonaguni monument (Japan)　Moeraki Boulders (New Zealand)

1 Where is the place located?
2 What can we see there now?
3 Why is the place so unusual?
4 Is the place natural or man-made?

5 If natural, how was it made?
6 If man-made, who built the place?
7 Why did they build it?

English in action
Agreeing and disagreeing

1 (3.17) **Listen and number the expressions in order. Then answer the question.**

Saying you agree

☐ I totally agree.

☐ Absolutely!

☐ You're right.

☐ That's so true.

Saying you disagree

☐ I totally disagree.

☐ I don't think so.

☐ 1 I'm not so sure about that.

☐ I don't agree.

What type of film do the boys decide to watch?

2 💡 **Read the statements. Do you agree or disagree? Write your answers. Use the expressions in Activity 1 to help you. Then practise with your partner.**

1 Horror stories are fun to read before you go to bed.   *I totally disagree.*

2 Watching videos is better than reading books.

3 Comics and graphic novels are only for young children.

4 There aren't any interesting programmes on TV.

5 Romance stories and films can be quite boring.

6 Science fiction stories are always about robots.

7 Adventure stories are the best thing to read.

8 Poetry books are boring for children.

Pronunciation

3 (3.18) 💬 **Listen and read. Do the expressions go up or down? Draw ↑ or ↓. Then practise with your partner.**

1 I totally disagree. ↓

2 That's so true.

3 I don't think you're right at all.

4 That's definitely not right.

5 I couldn't agree more.

6 I totally agree.

7 I'm not so sure about that.

8 Definitely!

Literacy: detective stories

Reading

Words in context

1 **Read and complete the sentences.**

advertisement   assistant   ~~business~~   league   plan   tunnel

1 My brother is starting a new ___*business*___ . He's going to sell computers.

2 We need to get organised and make a _____ for our trip to Istanbul next weekend.

3 There's a long, underwater _____ that goes from the UK to France.

4 Did you see that _____ for jeans on TV? It was really funny!

5 Manchester United and Arsenal play in the same football _____ .

6 Many people need an _____ to help them with their job.

2 **Read the detective story on Pupil's Book page 40 again. Who says the following sentences? Write.**

1 ___*Holmes*___ 'Mr Wilson is telling me a strange story.'

2 _____ 'I have a shop which isn't doing well.'

3 _____ 'We have to stop a thief – tonight!'

4 _____ 'That night, I found two men with Holmes in his flat.'

5 _____ 'You saved the bank tonight. You really are a great detective.'

6 _____ 'And you caught him, Holmes!'

Holmes   Merryweather

Wilson   Watson

3 **Read the sentences and circle *T* (true) or *F* (false). Then explain your answers.**

1 Sherlock Holmes is a large man with red hair.   T / (F)

Mr Wilson is a large man with red hair.

4 There was £30,000 in a room under Mr Wilson's shop.   T / F

_____

2 Mr Spaulding showed Mr Wilson a strange advertisement.   T / F

_____

5 Officer Jones was helping Mr Merryweather protect the bank.   T / F

_____

3 Mr Wilson's shop was called The League of Redheads.   T / F

_____

6 John Clay and Mr Wilson made the tunnel to the bank.   T / F

_____

4 **Work in groups. Discuss what a good detective should and shouldn't do and make notes. Then share your ideas with the class.**

ask questions   be hard-working   be friendly   believe everyone   forget anything
watch people   talk too much   be shy   take notes   think quickly   be polite

Literacy: detective stories

Writing

1 **Rewrite the sentences with correct punctuation for reported speech.**

1 you don't need to call the police cried the young man

'You don't need to call the police,' cried the young man.

2 it's quite late said Amy and we should probably go

_____

3 when did you guess the identity of the thief asked Watson

_____

4 don't move shouted the police officer you're under arrest

_____

5 this is the best birthday party I've ever had smiled Jack

_____

> **tip** **Writing**
>
> **Punctuation for speech**
> Make sure you use the correct punctuation for speech.
> *'Max and Leo,' he said to the brothers, 'where were you last night?'*
> Remember to start a new line for each speaker.

2 **Plan a detective story.**

| Choose a setting and characters that are interesting. | → |

| Write a good beginning that explains the mystery and makes us want to read the story. | → |

| Write a middle that is exciting and has suspense throughout the story to keep people interested. | → |

| Write an ending that solves the mystery and answers all the questions. | → |

3 **Now write your story.**

4 **Check your work. Tick (✓) the steps when you have done them.**

Have I described the setting and the characters? ☐

Have I given the story a good plot and solved the mystery at the end? ☐

Have I created interest and suspense? ☐

Have I used the correct punctuation for reported speech? ☐

1 **Look at the pictures and write the types of books.**

 1    2    3    4    5    6

fantasy _____ _____ _____ _____ _____

2 **Write sentences. Replace the words in bold with adjectives from Pupil's Book page 37.**

1 Emily is a **very friendly** person.

Emily is a popular person.

2 That's a **very beautiful** house.

_____

3 We had to walk up a **high** hill.

_____

4 The hotel room was **really small**.

_____

5 I had a **bad** feeling about the exam.

_____

6 These pictures you've drawn are **really pretty**.

_____

3 **Write the sentences with reported speech.**

1 Tom said, 'I have to tidy my room.'   *Tom said that he had to tidy his room.*

2 Lucy told me, 'My mum's a doctor.' _____

3 They said, 'We don't like comics.' _____

4 Dan told me, 'You're late.' _____

5 Ana said, 'I want to go home.' _____

4 **Write sentences in the Present and Past simple passive.**

1 that castle / build / in 1545

That castle was built in 1545.

2 Italy / know / for its delicious food

_____

3 the first jeans / made / for workers

_____

4 many cities / locate / near rivers

_____

5 the palace / not / visit / by many people

_____

6 my books / not / damage / by the fire

_____

Self-evaluation

5 **Answer the questions about your work in Unit 3.**

1 How was your work in this unit? Choose.   ☐ OK   ☐ Good   ☐ Excellent

2 Which lesson was your favourite? _____

3 Which parts of the unit were difficult for you? _____

4 What new things can you talk about now? _____

5 How can you work and learn better in the next unit? _____

Get ready for...

A2 Key for Schools Listening Part 3

 1 Read the task carefully. Make sure you know what you have to do.

Try! **2** 🎧 3.20 Listen and choose the correct answer. Then explain your answer.

Betty says that
A horror stories are boring.
B she loves fantasy stories.
C she doesn't like mysteries.

_____

_____

_____

_____

Do! **3** 🎯 🎧 3.21 For each question, choose the correct answer. You will hear Emma talking to a shop assistant about books.

tip Exam

Listen the second time and check all your answers carefully, focusing on specific information.

1 Emma wants to buy a book for
 A her friend.
 B her cousin.
 C her brother.

2 Michael's birthday party is
 A tomorrow.
 B this Friday.
 C on Saturday.

3 Michael isn't interested in
 A science fiction.
 B fantasy novels.
 C horror stories.

4 Emma prefers to read
 A mysteries.
 B romance novels.
 C biographies.

5 Emma will probably buy
 A one book.
 B two books.
 C three books.

B1 Preliminary for Schools Reading Part 2

Think! **1** Read the task carefully. Make sure you know what you have to do.

Try! **2** Read the five descriptions of people in Activity 3. Find and write the words for each person. Tick (✓) the words relating to the books the people enjoy.

~~detective~~ fantasy scary fictional future poetry real romance ~~action~~ superheroes

Richard: _action_ ✓ _detective_ ☐   Helen: _____ ☐ _____ ☐

Betty: _____ ☐ _____ ☐   William: _____ ☐ _____ ☐

Oliver: _____ ☐ _____ ☐

Do! **3** 🎯 The people below all want to buy a book. Read the eight book reviews. Decide which book would be the most suitable for each person. Write the correct letter (A–H).

tip Exam

Read the five descriptions of the people and the eight texts carefully. Underline any matches between the descriptions and the texts.

New Books!

1 Richard ☐
Richard enjoys novels with lots of action and adventure, but he isn't a fan of mysteries or detective stories because he finds them too long and boring.

2 Betty ☐
Betty likes reading about people in the past and how they lived and thought, but only real stories. She isn't interested in fictional characters or events.

3 Oliver ☐
Oliver is studying to be a chef, so he's always looking for new ideas. He enjoys poetry, but he doesn't like poems about love and romance.

4 Helen ☐
Helen used to like fantasy when she was younger, but now she only reads science fiction, especially stories about future technology.

5 William ☐
William collects graphic novels about superheroes and their adventures. He isn't into horror stories or anything scary like that.

A Born to Sing?
Since he was a boy, George has dreamed of becoming a famous rock star, and now he's finally got a chance. After winning a talent show, George has been asked to join the famous band, Rock Monsters. But does George really have enough talent to be a star?

B Mega Men
Fans have waited almost two years for the Mega Men to return, but they definitely won't be disappointed. The artwork is better than ever and the first story of this new series brings back all of the most popular superheroes. There will also be a film version coming soon!

C Catherine the Great
Anyone who had studied Russia's most famous empress should read this new biography. It includes letters that Catherine sent to her friends, with her personal thoughts and feelings about the events she experienced. It's a fantastic book for anyone who loves history.

D Penny's Problem
Penny Banks has solved a lot of mysteries over the years, but this time she's got a problem. Someone has stolen the Red Diamond and all the clues point to her good friend, Nigel. But is Nigel really a criminal, or is someone playing a mysterious game?

E Tech Dreams
In the distant future, people won't go on holiday anymore. They'll connect to computers and dream of exciting places on the other side of the universe. But what will happen if one day the computers decide that people should keep on sleeping and never wake up?

F Romantic Rhymes
For those of you who enjoy good poetry, this new collection of love poems is the perfect addition to your library. There are poems from thirty different authors, from Shakespeare to the modern day, with biographical notes about each one of them.

G Fast and Fantastic
If you are bored of preparing the same old dishes, but you haven't got much time for cooking, then you need Paul Gaston's new collection of quick, easy-to-make meals. It includes family favourites as well as ideas for a romantic dinner for two! Pick up a copy today!

H Into Zandor
Idaho Johnson, the rainforest explorer, has been in many dangerous situations, and he's always survived. But has he made a mistake this time? No one has ever visited the Lost City of Zandor and returned to talk about it. Will Idaho be the first one, or will he disappear, too?

Mateo's Learning Club

Language booster 1

1 **After you read** Read the text on Pupil's Book page 44 again. Write *True* or *False*.

1 This website is useful for tourists. _____*True*_____
2 It is written by tour guides. _____
3 The Terracotta Army was found more than 2,000 years ago. _____
4 Matias likes a historical place in his city. _____
5 The Banpo Bridge in Seoul is older than Big Ben in London. _____
6 You can watch light shows at Big Ben. _____

2 Read and match.

clock tower   fountain   monument   statue   ~~tour guide~~   tourist

1 This person shows people on holiday around a place. _____*tour guide*_____
2 This is a model of a person or animal, usually made of stone. _____
3 This person is visiting a place on holiday. _____
4 This is a thing where water is pushed up into the air and falls again. _____
5 This is a thing we build to remember people or events in history. _____
6 You can look up at this thing to tell the time. _____

3 Order the letters to complete the sentences.

1 This roundabout is very big. It's _____*huge*_____ (ehug).
2 A lot of people visit this museum. It's very _____(lpuropa).
3 This hill is very hard to climb because it's so _____(tepse).
4 This railway station is very small. It's _____(ytni).
5 There's no light in this hotel. It's _____(rakd).
6 The view from here is very beautiful. It's _____(rgoseugo).

4 Write your own tip to add to the website on Pupil's Book page 44.

_____ My favourite place in my city is _____
_____ It's _____
_____ I like it because _____
_____ _____

5 (LB1.2) **Read and listen to the dialogue on Pupil's Book page 45 again. Complete Sara and Mark's schedule for the weekend.**

Saturday

Morning: (1) _market under the clock tower_

Afternoon:
(2) _____

Sunday

Morning:
(3) _____

Afternoon:
(4) _____

6 **Write suggestions.**

1 we / ask / at / the tourist information centre?

Shall we ask at the tourist information centre?

2 I / carry / your luggage?

_____

3 we / climb / the monument?

_____

4 we / meet / at / the fountain?

_____

5 I / call / a taxi?

_____

6 we / take / the bus?

_____

7 (LB1.3) **Complete the dialogue with the words below. Then listen and check.**

minute   next   shall   ~~want~~   what

Tom: Holly, let's decide where we're going to go in London tomorrow.

Holly: OK. If you **(1)** _want_ .

Tom: Shall we climb up The Monument in the morning?

Holly: Yes, good idea. I think that'll be interesting. What **(2)** _____?

Tom: How about doing some shopping in the afternoon?

Holly: Oh, no. I hate shopping.

Tom: OK, **(3)** _____ else? Let me think … Well, **(4)** _____ we do a treasure hunt? I've got a new treasure hunt app on my phone!

Holly: Yes, that sounds fun!

Tom: Cool! I can't wait! So, are you ready for some lunch yet?

Holly: In a **(5)** _____ . I just want to finish my chapter.

8 **Complete the suggestions for things to do with a friend on a Saturday.**

Shall we _____ ?

Yes, good idea. What next?

How about _____ ?

Oh, no! I hate _____ .

OK. What else?

Well, shall we _____ ?

Yes, that sounds _____ !

 Our planet

Vocabulary

1 **Read and circle the correct options.**

1 At our school, we **waste** / **recycle** / **destroy** paper, plastic, glass and other materials.

2 If we don't **change** / **plant** / **protect** the environment, we'll have problems in the future.

3 A lot of people **switch** / **waste** / **save** energy by leaving on lights all the time.

4 Scientists think people's activities are causing **global** / **climate** / **environment** warming.

5 We're learning about climate **energy** / **water** / **change** in Science at school.

6 Air **pollution** / **rubbish** / **waste** from cars and factories is very bad for the environment.

2 **Look, read and complete the sentences.**

1 We mustn't ___destroy the rainforests___ .

2 Please _____ the _____ when you go out.

3 Try to _____ when you brush your teeth.

4 Do you _____ in the street?

5 People need to _____ .

6 It's a good idea to _____ in your garden.

 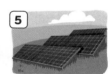 

3 **Read the *I'm learning* box. Then read and complete the sentences with verbs for protecting our planet. There may be more than one correct answer.**

> **I'm learning**
>
> **Using verbs with different objects**
> We can learn a verb in a phrase and then use it with different objects.
> *Please switch off the lights.*
> *Please switch off the TV.*

1 Could you please ___pick up___ those bottles and put them in the bin?

2 If we cut down too many trees, it will _____ the forests.

3 We need to _____ our rivers and lakes from water pollution.

4 People often _____ solar energy in sunny countries.

5 You shouldn't _____ paper. Always write on both sides.

6 My parents are going to _____ some flowers in the garden.

4 **Write five or more sentences about what you and your family do to help the environment.**

1 (4.4) **Read and match the two halves of the sentences from the dialogue on Pupil's Book page 50. Then listen and check.**

1 There's a competition to

2 What can we do to

3 We need to switch off lights and

4 Can we do anything to

5 So we need to

6 We must go or we'll

a turn off computers when we leave a room.

b be late for our next lesson.

c save energy then?

d let everyone know about the competition.

e see which school can save the most energy.

f save water?

2 **Read the dialogue again and circle T (true) or F (false). Then explain your answers.**

1 Mei suggests taking part in a competition.   **T / F**   *Mateo suggests it.*

2 Alex asks about ways they can save energy.   **T / F**   _____

3 Alex wants to throw away the plastic bottles.   **T / F**   _____

4 Mateo found the hot water running in the kitchen.   **T / F**   _____

5 Mateo doesn't want people's suggestions.   **T / F**   _____

6 Mei tells Mateo to turn off the computer.   **T / F**   _____

3 (4.5) **Read and complete the dialogues with the correct expressions. Then listen and check.**

Brilliant! × 2   I know! × 2   Me too! × 2

1 A: I think recycling is very important.

   B: ___*Me too!*___ I recycle as much as possible.

2 A: What can you do to save water at home?

   B: _____ I can have shorter showers.

3 A: I'm writing a blog about clean energy.

   B: _____ You're so creative!

4 B: How can we use less paper at school?

   A: _____ We can do our homework online!

5 A: I want to look for a new tablet.

   B: _____ My tablet is broken. Let's go shopping!

6 A: Look! I got full marks in our Science test!

   B: _____ You're so clever.

4 **Work in pairs. Write another dialogue for each expression. Then act out the dialogues.**

Grammar

Modal verbs: *should, must, need to*

1 🎧 (4.8) **Listen and tick (✓) the correct sentences.**

1 ☐ **a** Paul must hand in the report on Monday.

☑ **b** Paul needn't make a poster.

2 ☐ **a** Nina should stop watching videos now.

☐ **b** Nina needs to be home at six o'clock.

3 ☐ **a** Sam mustn't forget his Maths book.

☐ **b** Sam shouldn't tidy up his bedroom today.

4 ☐ **a** Ana mustn't go to the cinema today.

☐ **b** Ana needs to ask her parents for money.

2 **Read and circle the correct modal verbs.**

1 We **shouldn't** / **(need to)** / **mustn't** use more electric cars to reduce air pollution.

2 All the students **need** / **must** / **shouldn't** do their homework. It's very important.

3 People **shouldn't** / **need to** / **must** leave the lights on when they go out.

4 You **needn't** / **should** / **mustn't** waste energy because it's bad for the environment.

5 We **must** / **needn't** / **should** print so many things on paper. It's a waste!

6 She **should** / **must** / **need** have a shower instead a bath because it uses less water.

3 **Re-write each sentence so that it means the same as the first sentence. Use the affirmative or negative form of the modal verb in brackets.**

1 Don't throw rubbish on the ground. (should)
You shouldn't throw rubbish on the ground.

2 We have to stop cutting down trees. (must)
_____

3 I don't have to tidy my room today. (need)
_____

4 Jo, please don't shout in the classroom. (must)
_____

5 Why don't you put on a sweater? (should)
_____

6 People should recycle more plastic. (need)
_____

4 💬 **Order the words to make sentences. Tick (✓) the sentences you agree with. Then compare your answers with your partner.**

1 lights people off switch should
People should switch off lights. ☐

2 protect must the environment everyone
_____ ☐

3 people water needn't save
_____ ☐

4 energy more to should we waste try
_____ ☐

5 new must lots people trees of plant
_____ ☐

6 use lots to need paper of we
_____ ☐

7 people rainforests the shouldn't destroy
_____ ☐

8 street mustn't the in pick up we rubbish
_____ ☐

» Grammar reference, page 121

1 **After you read** **Read the diary on Pupil's Book page 52 again. Number the events in order.**

- [ ] **a** Jake's dad said he shouldn't worry.
- [ ] **b** It stopped raining the following morning.
- [ ] **c** All the tourists went to the dining room.
- [1] **d** Jake woke up early and watched the big storm.
- [ ] **e** The lights went out and the room was dark.
- [ ] **f** Jake's dad told him that the storm was a hurricane.
- [ ] **g** The hurricane flooded a local harbour.
- [ ] **h** Everyone got down on the floor and waited.

2 **Answer the questions. Use complete sentences.**

1 Why did Jake get up early?

He got up early because the storm woke him up.

2 How did he know about the hurricane?

_____

3 Where did he spend the first morning?

_____

4 Why did people go to the dining room?

_____

5 What did everyone do with all the furniture?

_____

6 What did Jake's dad tell him to do when it went dark?

_____

3 **Read the *Work with words* box. Then read and complete the sentences with a phrasal verb with *get*.**

> **Work with words**
>
> **Phrasal verbs with *get***
>
> We can combine the verb *get* with prepositions to make phrasal verbs.
>
> *get + up = **get up***
>
> *Why did he **get up**?*
>
> *He **got up** because the storm woke him up.*

1 If there's an earthquake you should ___*get under*___ a table.

2 Please _____ the car. We have to leave now.

3 How did your cat _____ that tree?

4 You must _____ of the house if there is a fire.

5 How fast can you _____ the stairs to the front door in an emergency?

6 My father used a ladder to _____ the roof.

4 **Write sentences using the six phrasal verbs from Activity 3.**

Vocabulary and Grammar

1 Label the pictures.

snowstorm _____ _____

_____ _____ _____

2 🎧 (4.12) Listen and tick (✓) the extreme weather that you hear. There is more than one answer.

1
- ☐ gale
- ☐ tsunami
- ☐ tornado
- ☐ flood
- ✓ hurricane
- ☐ snowstorm

2
- ☐ volcano
- ☐ heatwave
- ☐ avalanche
- ☐ forest fire
- ☐ drought
- ☐ thunder and lightning

3 🎧 (4.13) Listen again. Complete the text.

¹ _____Hurricanes_____ and ² _____
have strong winds that blow in circles.
A hurricane is ³ _____ than a
tornado and it also lasts longer. A
⁴ _____ is a ⁵ _____
wind, but it doesn't blow in circles.
A ⁶ _____ is when the
weather is very ⁷ _____.
A ⁸ _____ is when it doesn't
⁹ _____ for a long time.
That can be dangerous because
everything gets dry and there could be
a ¹⁰ _____.

Reported questions and commands

4 Read and complete the reported questions.

1  Are you busy, Tom? Dan

2  Where do penguins live? Lori

1 Dan asked *Tom if he was busy.*

2 Lori asked _____

3  Does a tornado last a long time? Celine

4  When is it summer in Australia? Ali

3 Celine _____

4 Ali _____

5  Is a tsunami very dangerous? Diego

6  What can I do to help? Olya

5 Diego _____

6 Olya _____

5 Write reported commands.

1 Adam ➜ us: 'Get under the table!'
Adam told us to get under the table.

2 My parents ➜ me: 'Don't be late.'
_____

3 Camila ➜ her sister: 'Stop wearing my clothes!'
_____

4 My friends ➜ me: 'Don't buy more shoes!'
_____

5 We ➜ Maria: 'Join the basketball team!'
_____

6 I ➜ everyone: 'Don't call me at night.'
_____

>>> Grammar reference, page 121

1 **After you read** Read the text on Pupil's Book page 54 again. What do the sentences describe? Write.

1 These animals eat mostly one type of plant material.   _giant pandas_

2 It's getting smaller every year because of global warming.   _____

3 These animals live in very high, warm areas of Africa.   _____

4 There'll be more of these things if our planet gets hotter.   _____

5 They are large animals that live in very cold climates.   _____

6 This doesn't grow very quickly and that could be problem.   _____

2 Answer the questions. Use complete sentences.

1 What could be dangerous for animals in the future?

   Climate change could be dangerous for animals in the future.

2 Why is sea ice so important for polar bears' survival?

   _____

3 Why do some polar bears have problems in the summer?

   _____

4 What will happen if there isn't enough bamboo in China?

   _____

5 How many mountain gorillas are there in the world now?

   _____

6 Why can mountain gorillas survive if the Earth gets hotter?

   _____

3 (4.15) Listen to a report about another endangered animal. Complete the notes.

The Monarch butterfly

We can find them in
¹ _North America_ . They are
black and ² _____ with
³ _____ spots.
Monarchs get their food from ⁴ _____
and ⁵ _____ .
They fly ⁶ _____ in winter and travel about
⁷ _____ kilometres from Canada to Mexico.
Monarchs will have problems if winters become
⁸ _____ and ⁹ _____ .
People are also destroying the ¹⁰ _____
where monarchs live.

4 📶 Work in groups. Choose one of the endangered animals in the box and find answers to the questions. Then make a poster about your endangered animal.

> Amur leopard
> Giant Chinese salamander
> Northern right whale
> Javan rhino   Sumatran orangutan

1 Where does the animal live?
2 What does the animal look like?
3 Where does it get its food from?
4 How does climate change affect this animal?
5 What other problems does this animal have?

English in action
Giving advice

1 🎧 (4.18) **Read and complete the dialogue. Then listen and check.**

> **a** Why don't you look for one online? **d** ~~Really? That sounds interesting.~~
> **b** I think you should try to recycle more, too. **e** Perhaps you ought to write a blog.
> **c** If I were you, I would join a nature club. **f** You could always pick up rubbish.

Boy: I want to do something to help the environment.

Girl: ¹ _d Really? That sounds interesting._

Boy: Do you have any ideas?

Girl: ² _____

Boy: Oh! I don't know any clubs like that.

Girl: ³ _____

Boy: Sure. I'll look this afternoon. What else?

Girl: Hmm. ⁴ _____

Boy: Yes, I often pick things up. Any other advice?

Girl: ⁵ _____

Boy: OK. I recycle, but I could do more. Anything else?

Girl: You write well. ⁶ _____

Boy: A blog about the environment? What a great idea!

2 ✳ **Read the statements. Write advice. Then act out the dialogues with your partner.**

1 'I want to do something fun this weekend. The weather is going to be nice.'

I think _you should have a picnic at the beach._ _____

2 'I'm not getting doing very well in Maths this year.'

Perhaps _____

3 'I don't know what to get my mother for her birthday.'

If I _____

4 'I have too much free time. I think I need a new hobby.'

Why don't _____

Pronunciation

3 🎧 (4.19) 💬 **Listen and read the sentences. Look at the <u>underlined</u> words and circle the letters we don't pronounce. Then practise with your partner.**

1 They <u>mus(t)n't</u> call me today.

2 We <u>shouldn't</u> read that book.

3 I <u>couldn't</u> do my homework.

4 You <u>should</u> tidy your room.

5 She <u>mustn't</u> leave the room.

6 Please <u>could</u> you turn off the lights?

Literacy: reports

Reading

1 **Read the definitions and write the words.**

<del>foundation</del>   tonne   piece   business   government   end up

1 This is an organisation that provides money to help people.   _foundation_

2 This is something that is part of something bigger and more complete.   _____

3 This is a group of people who lead a town, region or country.   _____

4 This is a unit of weight that is the same as 1,000 kilograms.   _____

5 This is when an object is in a particular place after someone has done something to it.   _____

6 This is an organisation that sells products or services for money.   _____

2 **Read the report on Pupil's Book page 56 again. Read and complete the sentences with two words.**

1 Plastic in the sea will   _cause problems_   for the whole planet in the future.

2 About 95% of the plastic we make is _____.

3 Eight million tonnes of plastic goes into the ocean _____.

4 Pieces of plastic in the ocean _____ for fish and other animals.

5 Plastic pollution _____ a serious problem in the future.

6 The world's _____ is serious. We must protect our oceans.

today	2050
311 million tonnes	1,124 million tonnes
1:5	>1:1

3 **Answer the questions. Use complete sentences.**

1 Who wrote the report about the pollution?

The Ellen MacArthur Foundation wrote the report.

2 How much more plastic do we make now than we did 50 years ago?

_____

3 How much plastic goes into the ocean every minute?

_____

4 What causes problems for seals and turtles?

_____

5 Why is the report important?

_____

6 What type of plastic should businesses always use?

_____

4 **Work in groups. Choose one of the problems in the box. Discuss the questions and make notes. Then share your ideas with the class.**

air pollution   endangered animals
forest fires   water shortage

1 Who and what does the problem affect?

2 Why do you think it's an important problem?

3 What can countries do to solve the problem?

4 What can you and your friends do to help?

Literacy: reports

Writing

tip Writing

while and *however*
To compare two different things, use *while* or *however*.

1 Read and complete the sentences with *while* or *however*.

1 My sister says she wants to help the environment. ___However___ , she doesn't pick up her rubbish

2 In our survey we found that 52% of students recycle rubbish _____ 8% turn off lights

3 27 students say they save water at home. _____ only 6 students say they plant trees.

2 Look at the diagrams. Answer the questions.

Is it important to save water?

Yes: 77%
No: 18%
Don't know: 5%

What's the best way to save water?

Take a quick shower: 46%
Turn off the water when you're brushing your teeth: 28%
Have a garden that doesn't need much water: 15%
Don't use the toilet as a rubbish bin: 9%
Don't know: 2%

Survey of 386 students, aged between 11 and 14

1 What do the diagrams show?

They show students' answers to a survey
about saving water.

2 How many students did the survey?

_____

3 How old were the students?

_____

4 How many students think saving water is important?

_____

5 How many ways to save water are listed?

_____

6 Which two ideas are the most popular?

_____

3 💡 Study the two diagrams and plan a report about the survey results.

Include a clear title. _____

Write an introduction. What do the diagrams show? What was the survey about? _____

Explain the two diagrams. Use *firstly* and *secondly* and also use *while* and *however* to compare two different things. _____

Use formal language. Don't use contractions of verbs. _____

Write a conclusion and explain why the survey is interesting. Give reasons. Don't include your own opinions. Use the facts from the survey. _____

4 Now write your report about the survey.

5 Check your work. Tick (✓) the steps when you have done them.

Have I written a good introduction? ☐

Have I used full forms and formal language? ☐

Have I presented facts and not opinions? ☐

Have I used expressions to explain the results? ☐

1 Read and complete the sentences.

> destroy   plant   use   recycle
> switch off   ~~waste~~

Protect
the planet!

1 Please don't ___waste___ energy!

2 People should _____ new trees.

3 Please _____ plastic, paper and glass.

4 We mustn't _____ the rainforests.

5 Remember to _____ the lights.

6 Everyone should _____ renewable energy.

2 Unscramble the weather words to complete the sentences.

1 When there's a ___hurricane___ (riruhance) you should stay indoors. There are strong winds and a lot of rain.

2 The firefighters worked through the night to put out the _____ (erif orfest).

3 It's too hot for me today. I hope this _____ (vewathea) finishes soon. I prefer cooler weather.

4 Look out of the window. There's a _____ (sstrwoomn), so you can't go outside. We'll build a snowman later.

5 Wow, look at that photo of the wave on the ocean! It's a huge _____ (namitsu).

3 Read and complete the sentences with the correct form of the modal verbs.

1 We ___shouldn't waste___ so much energy in our homes. (should / waste)

2 Everyone _____ to protect our planet. (must / help)

3 I _____ new clothes every week. (need / buy)

4 Children _____ how to save water. (should / learn)

5 You _____ plastic in the ocean. (must / throw)

6 Campers _____ careful with fire. (need / be)

4 Write reported questions and commands.

1 Tom → Ana: 'Are you tired?'

Tom asked Ana if she was tired.

2 Dad → Paul: 'Switch off the light.'

_____

3 Ali → Zac: 'When is the concert?'

_____

4 Sue → Ben: 'What do you want?'

_____

5 Amy → Bo: 'Do you like apples?'

_____

6 Mum → Tamar: 'Don't be late.'

_____

Self-evaluation

5 Answer the questions about your work in Unit 4.

1 How was your work in this unit? Choose. ☐ OK ☐ Good ☐ Excellent

2 Which lesson was your favourite? _____

3 Which parts of the unit were difficult for you? _____

4 What new things can you talk about now? _____

5 How can you work and learn better in the next unit? _____

Get ready for...

A2 Key for Schools Listening Part 4

 1 Read the task carefully. Make sure you know what you have to do.

 2 Listen and choose the correct sentence. Then explain your answer.

1 A Holly uses a lot of renewable energy.
  B Holly isn't going to have baths anymore.
  C Holly uses less water to brush her teeth.

2 A Michael is going to recycle the bottle.
  B Michael is going to throw the bottle into the bin.
  C Michael's mum will reuse the bottle.

Do! **3** Listen. For each question, choose the correct answer.

1 You will hear a man talking to his daughter, Katy. Why does he call her to the living room?

  A She didn't tidy up the living room.
  B She forgot to switch off the TV.
  C She wasn't doing her homework.

2 You will hear a teacher, Ms Daniels, talking to her students. What did she ask them to do?

  A Read an article about climate change.
  B Answer questions about air pollution.
  C Write a text about global warming.

3 You will hear a boy and a girl talking about a group. How can the boy learn more?

  A Read the posters in the park.
  B Go to the meeting in the spring.
  C Look at the blog on the internet.

4 You will hear a boy doing a presentation. How much of our planet's water can we drink?

  A Ninety-seven percent.
  B Three percent.
  C Thirty-nine percent.

tip **Exam**

Listen for the first time to get the gist and choose the best option for each question.

A2 Key for Schools Reading and Writing Part 7

Think! **1** Read the task carefully. Make sure you know what you have to do.

Try! **2** Look at the picture. Answer the questions.

1 Where was the girl?

She was at the bus stop.

2 What was she doing?

3 What was the man doing?

Do! **3** 🎯 Look at the three pictures. Write the story shown in the pictures. Write 35 words or more.

tip Exam

Ask yourself what is happening in each picture. How are the events connected?

Lesson

Adventure sports

Vocabulary

1 **Write the sports.**

1 surfboarding

2 w_____

3 d_____

4 g_____

5 s_____

6 r_____

2 **Read and complete the sentences.**

golf   horse-riding   ice hockey   jogging   kite surfing   motor-racing

1 I'm learning to play _____golf_____ now. It isn't easy to hit the ball correctly.

2 I love the beach on windy days because I can go _____.

3 I need new trainers for _____. I go every day and I do about five kilometres.

4 I often watch _____ on TV. My favourite event is Formula One.

5 I love ice skating and I enjoy team sports, so _____ is my favourite sport.

6 I often go _____ at my grandparents' farm. I love animals!

3 **Read the *I'm learning* box. Then complete the table about sports from this lesson.**

> **I'm learning**
>
> **Classifying sports**
> We can classify sports into different groups by where we do them or who we do them with.
> *Golf is an outdoor sport.*
> *Jogging is an individual sport.*
> *Surfboarding is a water sport.*

indoor sports	golf,
outdoor sports	
water sports	
snow/ice sports	
team sports	
individual sports	

4 **Write five sentences about other sports. Where do you do them and who with?**

54 fifty-four

1 (5.4) **Read and complete the sentences from the dialogue on Pupil's Book page 62. Who said them? Write. Then listen and check.**

always uses   enjoying yourself   hurts himself   let's go   playing squash   ~~rock climbing~~

1 _____Mei_____   I fell when I was _____rock climbing_____ and I hurt myself.

2 _____   My sister cut herself when she was _____ last week!

3 _____   I don't want to stop you from _____.

4 _____   That's too young. What if he _____?

5 _____   He _____ a helmet and wears special clothes.

6 _____   Come on, _____ or we'll be late for PE.

2 **Read the dialogue again and circle _T_ (true) or _F_ (false). Then explain your answers.**

1 Sophia thinks extreme sports are good for children.   T /(F)

She thinks that children shouldn't do
extreme sports.

2 Mei is sure that she can go rock climbing quite soon.   T / F

_____

3 Mei's cousin started playing squash when he was four.   T / F

_____

4 Mei thinks that children need to learn about danger.   T / F

_____

5 Sophia says that she doesn't want to go to PE.   T / F

_____

3 (5.5) **Read and complete the dialogues with the correct expressions. Then listen and check.**

(I suppose so.) x 2   (I told you so!) x 2   (Not really.) x 2

1 **A:** Are you OK?

  B: ¹ ___Not really.___ Someone took my cycling helmet today.

  A: Did you leave it on your bike?

  B: Yes, but only for a few minutes.

  A: I've always said that you shouldn't leave it on your bike. ² _____

  B: I know. And it was brand new!

  A: You really have to be more careful.

  B: ³ _____

2 **A:** Mum! I passed all my exams!

  B: I knew you could do it. ⁴ _____

  A: Yes, you did!

  B: I have an idea. Are you busy tomorrow at lunch time?

  A: ⁵ _____ What are you thinking?

  B: We can go out for lunch to celebrate!

  A: Great! Can we go out for pizza?

  B: Yes, ⁶ _____ It's your choice!

4 **Work in pairs. Write another dialogue for each expression. Then act out the dialogue.**

Grammar

Reflexive pronouns

1 (5.8) **Listen and circle the correct sentences.**

1 **a** The boy has hurt himself.

   b The boy was using a knife.

2 **a** The cat can't see itself.

   b The cat thinks it can see another cat.

3 **a** They boy would prefer to make a pizza.

   b They're making lunch themselves.

4 **a** The girl isn't happy with herself.

   b The girl says the test was difficult.

2 **Write the reflexive pronouns.**

Singular	Plural
1 I → _myself_	**6** we → _____
2 you → _____	**7** you → _____
3 he → _____	**8** they → _____
4 she → _____	
5 it → _____	

3 **Read and circle the correct pronouns.**

1 I often write notes to **me** / **myself** so I won't forget to do important things.

2 We called Sam and told **him** / **himself** to bring some music for the party.

3 Police officers must prepare **them** / **themselves** for emergencies.

4 Have your ever found **you** / **yourself** in a difficult situation at school?

5 You should call **us** / **ourselves** if you're going to arrive late.

6 No one knows **you** / **yourselves** better than your friends and family.

4 **Read and complete the sentences with the reflexive pronouns from Activity 2.**

1 'I taught ___myself___ to play the guitar by watching videos', said Miguel.

2 'Why didn't you and your brother cook _____ some dinner?', asked Mum.

3 'My baby sister is only one year old', said Anne, and she's just started teaching _____ to walk.'

4 'Tom and I met at a party', said Azra. 'We introduced _____ and started talking'.

5 'Our dog hurt _____ when it was playing in the garden', said Paul.

6 'Are your friends enjoying _____ at the party?', asked Dad.

7 The teacher asked Ivan, 'In what job do you see _____ in the future?'

8 Ben sometimes talks to _____ when he's thinking about a problem.

5 **Answer the questions. Write complete sentences.**

1 How well do you think you know yourself?

_____

2 How do you and your friends enjoy yourselves?

_____

3 Where do you imagine yourself in the future?

_____

4 What can people do to take care of themselves?

_____

6 **Work with your partner. Ask them the questions from Activity 5 and write their answers in your notebook.**

»» Grammar reference, page 122

 **Book Club** 5

1 After you read Read the adventure story on Pupil's Book page 64 again. Match the two parts of the sentences.

1 After the children had eaten breakfast,   **a** they started walking across the valley.

2 After they had packed some food,   **b** she used it to call for help.

3 After they'd walked across the valley,   **c** they looked in their guidebook.

4 After the man had hurt his foot,   **d** they took him to a nearby hospital.

5 After Yasmin had turned on her phone,   **e** he couldn't climb back up the cliff.

6 After the people had rescued the man,   **f** they decided to climb up the hill.

2 Answer the questions. Use complete sentences.

1 Where did the children decide to camp?   *They decided to camp near a small wood.*

2 Why did they want to wake up early? _____

3 Whose compass did Fiona bring? _____

4 Why did Mark stop walking to the beach? _____

5 How long did they wait for the helicopter? _____

6 What will the man remember next time? _____

3 Read the *Work with words* box. Make compound adjectives with the words in the box.

> **Work with words**
>
> **Compound adjectives**
> Some adjectives are formed from two words joined by a hyphen (-).
> old + fashioned = **old-fashioned**
> My dad has an **old-fashioned** radio from the 1960s.

cold famous ~~hour~~ made speaking winning

1 nine-*hour*   4 English-_____

2 home-_____   5 prize-_____

3 ice-_____   6 world-_____

4 Read and complete the sentences with the compound adjectives from Activity 3.

1 We took a ___*nine-hour*___ bus ride from Cordoba to Buenos Aires.

2 The USA is an _____ country.

3 Shakira is a _____ singer from Colombia.

4 I felt really hot so I drank an _____ glass of lemonade.

5 My aunt has a _____ dog. It has won lots of competitions.

6 I love my mum's _____ chocolate cake. It's delicious!

5 Write five sentences with compound adjectives you know.

Vocabulary and Grammar

1 Look, read and complete.

The cows are in the __field__.

You can watch the _____ in the morning.

I love swimming in the _____.

The house is next to a small _____.

You can watch the _____ in the evening.

Our town is located in a beautiful _____.

2 🎧 5.13 Listen. In which dialogue do you hear these words? Write 1 or 2. There are two words you do not need.

directions	
north	east
south *1*	west
places	
bay	valley
field	wood
things	
scenery	sunset
sunrise	tide

Past perfect

3 Read and complete the sentences with the Past perfect form of the verbs in the box.

~~check~~   eat   leave   start   take   watch

1 After I __had checked__ my compass, I walked north.

2 My friends and I _____ the sunrise before we had breakfast.

3 After Angela _____ some photos of the scenery, she posted them online.

4 The bus _____ before I noticed that I didn't have my backpack with me.

5 After the campers _____ the fire, they cooked burgers for dinner.

6 Max _____ his lunch before he started hiking back home.

4 Read the text. Then write sentences in the Past perfect.

Ela arrived at the beach. Then, she went for a swim. Then, she put up her umbrella. Next, she read a magazine. Then, she ate a sandwich. After that, she took some photos.

1 (after / beach / swim) _After Ela had arrived at the beach, she went for a swim._

2 (after / swim / umbrella) _____

3 (before / umbrella / magazine) _____

4 (after / read / eat) _____

5 (before / sandwich / photos) _____

⟩⟩ Grammar reference, page 122

1 **After you read** **Read the text on Pupil's Book page 66 again. Read and complete the sentences. Write one word in each space.**

1 Underwater hockey is a water ___*sport*___ that is played in many different ___*countries*___ around the world.

2 A _____ of underwater hockey is 30 minutes long, with a 3-minute _____ in the middle.

3 In a tuna throwing competition, people _____ around very quickly before they _____ the fish as far as they can.

4 Fisherman often threw _____ off their boats when they had _____ too many.

5 Nicholas Kaufmann _____ cycleball in _____ in 1893.

6 Many countries take _____ in the cycleball World Cup, which is a game of _____ played on bikes.

2 **Read the sentences and circle _T_ (true) or _F_ (false). Then explain your answers.**

1 Underwater hockey matches are played by twelve people. (T) / F
There are two teams of six players.

2 Underwater hockey was first played in Australia. T / F
_____

3 Only fisherman can play the sport of tuna throwing. T / F
_____

4 People don't use real fish for tuna throwing nowadays. T / F
_____

5 Cycleball teams don't always have two players. T / F
_____

6 Cycleball players can move the ball with their hands. T / F
_____

3 **(5.15) Listen to a report about another unusual extreme sport. Complete the text.**

Zorbing is an unusual [1] ___*outdoor*___ sport that people do on hills in [2] _____. They get inside a big ball called a zorb. It's made of clear [3] _____. After they get inside, people roll down the hill as fast as they can. Zorbs are usually about [4] _____ metres across and only one person can fit inside. Some people enjoy competing in zorb [5] _____ to see who is the fastest. Other people only go zorbing for [6] _____. You can go zorbing on [7] _____ like lakes and swimming pools. Does that sound [8] _____ to you?

4 **Work in groups. Choose one of the unusual sports in the box and find answers to the questions. Write about your unusual sport.**

bed racing   bossaball   cheese rolling   curling   ostrich racing   sepak takraw

1 Where do people play the sport?
2 What do the players have to do?
3 What is needed to play the sport?
4 What rules must people follow?
5 What do you think of the sport?

English in action
Asking and saying what you prefer

1 (5.18) **Read and complete the dialogue. Then listen and check.**

> **a** Should we play golf or squash?
> **b** Would you prefer to go horse-riding
> **c** There are so many activities we can do.
>
> **d** I think that sounds excellent!
> **e** I'd rather go kite surfing.
> **f** I'd rather play squash on day two,

Turi: I'm really looking forward to our beach holiday.

Leo: Me too! [1] *c There are so many activities we can do.*

Turi: So, on day one, would you rather go kite surfing or surfboarding?

Leo: Oh, that's easy! [2] _____ And you?

Turi: I agree with you. I've always wanted to try that.

Leo: Let's have a look at day two. [3] _____

Turi: I think we should play golf. I'm terrible at squash.

Leo: Really? [4] _____ but we can do different things.

Turi: What about day three?

Leo: Let's have a look. [5] _____ or go-karting?

Turi: Well, I've been go-karting before, so I'd prefer to try horse-riding.

Leo: [6] _____ I can't wait!

2 ☀ **Read and complete the dialogues with your own ideas. Then act out the dialogues with your partner.**

1 A: Should we play _____basketball_____
   or _____ ?
   B: I think we should _____ .

2 A: Would you rather _____
   or _____ ?
   B: I'd rather _____ .

3 A: Should we _____
   or _____ ?
   B: I think we should _____ .

4 A: Would you prefer to _____
   or _____ ?
   B: I'd prefer to _____ .

Pronunciation

3 (5.19) 💬 **Listen and match. Then listen and repeat. Then practise with your partner.**

1 I'd finished eating breakfast
2 After we'd cycled for an hour,
3 They'd checked their work
4 After I'd finished the housework,
5 We'd visited the whole museum
6 After they'd arrived in Ankara,

a before they gave it to the teacher.
b before we went to the gift shop.
c I played a computer game.
d they took a bus to the hotel.
e before I left home for school.
f we had a break to drink some water.

Words in context

1 **Read and complete the definitions.**

expert ~~gentle~~ perfect stunning terrific

1 Someone who is doing things in a nice, kind and careful way is _____ *gentle* _____ .
2 Something that is extremely beautiful or attactive is _____ .
3 Something that people say is excellent or wonderful is _____ .
4 Something that is done with special skills and information is _____ .
5 Something that is made with no problems or mistakes is _____ .

2 **Read the brochure on Pupil's Book page 68 again. Write the different holidays.**

1 You can see amazing wild animals in many different countries. *safari adventures*
2 You can visit mountainous places in the UK, Spain or Nepal. _____
3 You will go to places that are cold and icy most of the year. _____
4 You won't be travelling around with many other people. _____
5 You can do an extreme sport that you've never done before. _____

3 **Answer the questions. Use complete sentences.**

1 Where can people go to play a winter sport?   *People can go to Canada to play ice hockey.*

2 Where can you go to see tigers in their natural habitat? _____
3 Why are safari adventure groups usually quite small? _____
4 Where can new climbers get experience on easy hills? _____
5 Who helps to keep the climbing adventures safe? _____
6 Where must people go if they want to see penguins? _____

4 **Work in groups. Choose a place from the box and think of ideas for an adventure holiday you could do there. Use the questions to help you. Then share your ideas with the class.**

the Amazon Rainforest   the Canary Islands   Lake Baikal
the Sahara Desert   the Rocky Mountains

1 Where is the place located?
2 What's the weather like there?
3 What sports can you do there?

4 What other activities can you do?
5 What advice can you give people?

Literacy: brochures and adverts

Writing

tip Writing

Strong adjectives
Use strong adjectives in your writing. For example, don't use *nice* – use *excellent* or *brilliant*. Don't use *bad* – use *awful* or *terrible*. Use the word *really* before an adjective to make the adjective stronger.

1 **Rewrite the sentences with exciting adjectives.**

awful   brilliant   delicious
~~fantastic~~   great   terrible

1 We went to a <u>very nice</u> beach in Hawaii.   *We went to a fantastic beach in Hawaii.*

2 The weather was <u>very bad</u> the first day.   _____

3 I tried surfboarding and I had a <u>good</u> time.   _____

4 I liked the food in Hawaii. It was <u>nice</u>.   _____

5 You should visit Hawaii. It's a <u>good</u> place.   _____

6 The weather was <u>bad</u> so we couldn't go surfboarding.   _____

2 **Plan a brochure for an outdoor activity.**

Include a fun title for the brochure.   _____

Start the text with an interesting question.   _____

Use exciting adjectives to keep people interested.   _____

Use short paragraphs that people can read easily and use pronouns, e.g. *you* and *we*.   _____

Finish with an interesting comment so people remember what you are writing about.   _____

Add an exciting picture to get people's attention.   _____

3 **Now write your brochure.**

4 **Check your work. Tick (✓) the steps when you have done them.**

Have I included a fun title?   ☐

Have I used exciting words to make the text interesting?   ☐

Have I used short, easy-to-read paragraphs?

Have I finished with a sentence that people will remember?

1 Write the sports. What's the mystery word?

1	G	O	L	F			
2			U	A			
3		O			I		
4	I		E		O		E
5		A		E			I
6		O		E	I		I
7		O				I		I

The mystery word is _____.

2 Look at the island. Read and complete the sentences.

1 The _____field_____ is on the _____north_____ side of the island.

2 The _____ is on the _____ side of the island.

3 The _____ is on the _____ side of the island.

4 The _____ is on the _____ side of the island.

3 Read and complete the sentences with reflexive pronouns.

1 Did you and your friends teach ___yourselves___ to dance?

2 The girls ordered _____ a big pizza for dinner.

3 Mateo fell off his bicycle and hurt _____ yesterday.

4 My friend Sara is always telling _____ to work harder.

5 We really enjoyed _____ at the concert last week.

4 Write sentences in the Past perfect.

1 I brushed my teeth. I got dressed. (after)

After I had brushed my teeth, I got dressed.

2 The game ended. We went home. (before)

_____

3 Tom ate lunch. He washed up. (after)

_____

4 Everyone left. We tidied up. (before)

_____

5 You called. I read a book. (after)

_____

6 Amy did her homework. She went to bed. (before)

_____

Self-evaluation

5 Answer the questions about your work in Unit 5.

1 How was your work in this unit? Choose. ☐ OK ☐ Good ☐ Excellent

2 Which lesson was your favourite? _____

3 Which parts of the unit were difficult for you? _____

4 What new things can you talk about now? _____

5 How can you work and learn better in the next unit? _____

A2 Key for Schools Listening Part 5

Think! **1** Read the task carefully. Make sure you know what you have to do.

Try! **2** (5.22) Which sport has Oliver already tried? Listen and choose the correct picture. Then explain your answer.

A surfboarding

B water skiing

C kite surfing

Do! **3** (target) (5.23) For each question, choose the correct answer. You will hear Harry talking to Sophia about summer activities. What activity will each child do?

tip Exam

Note that all the words in each list are from the same lexical set. Listen and make sure you choose the best option for each person.

1 Harry ☐

2 Sophia ☐

3 George ☐

4 Emma ☐

5 Richard ☐

A rock climbing

B diving

C squash

D horse-riding

E water skiing

F mountain-biking

G jogging

H go-karting

B1 Preliminary for Schools Reading Part 3

tip Exam

Look at the questions one by one, and make sure you compare each answer option with the text before choosing your answer.

Think! ① **Read the task carefully. Make sure you know what you have to do.**

Try! ② **Read and choose the sentences with a similar meaning.**

1 I don't enjoy myself when I'm alone.
   A I like spending time by myself.
   B Being alone can be quite enjoyable.
   C I prefer doing things with other people.
   D People should leave me alone.

2 We rested when the sun had set.
   A The sun set and then we rested.
   B We were resting when the sun set.
   C After resting, we watched the sun set.
   D The sun hadn't set when we rested.

Do! ③ 🎯 **Read the text and questions below. For each question, choose the correct answer, A, B, C or D.**

mily Jefferson talks about er love of horse-riding

grew up on a small farm where I pent a lot of time around animals, but here's always been a special place in y heart for horses. They're amazing nimals with their own personalities, ust like people! I love spending time round them, and that's why I became professional rider when I finished chool.

entered my first horse-riding ompetition at the age of fifteen, but tarted riding a long time before hat, when I was only five. Over the ext fifteen years, I won lots of awards the UK and other countries. My avourite horse is called Spirit, but he's oo old for competitions now. That's K, because I stopped competing st year. Now I give lessons to young eople on my parents' farm. One day, d like to buy my own farm and start a orse-riding academy. It won't be easy, ut I've always enjoyed a challenge!

1 Emily thinks
   A small farms are amazing.
   B horses have special hearts.
   C all people should like horses.
   D all horses behave differently.

2 Emily says she
   A won fifteen awards for horse-riding.
   B started horse-riding when she was young.
   C always competed in the UK.
   D stopped horse-riding at the age of fifteen.

3 Emily would like to
   A teach her parents to horse-ride.
   B compete with Spirit again.
   C teach horse-riding on her own farm.
   D improve her horse-riding.

4 Which sentence is correct?
   A The professional horse-rider Emily Jefferson started her career at quite an early age.
   B For Emily Jefferson, there is nothing more exciting than watching a horse-riding competition.
   C In this article, Emily Jefferson explains how her family raised horses in the countryside and then started an academy.
   D After growing up in the countryside, Emily Jefferson moved to the city where she started competing as a horse-rider.

Spend or save?

Vocabulary

1 **Read the clues and complete the crossword.**

1 This is a piece of paper you get when you buy something.
2 This is a special price that is lower than usual.
3 This has already been used or worn by another person.
4 This is a line of people waiting for something.
5 This is a person who buys something in a shop.
6 This is the machine that adds up prices in shops.

1 R E C E I P T

2 **Read and complete the sentences.**

1 You can ___exchange___ those shoes if you haven't worn them.
2 I'm not old enough to have a _____ so I always pay in cash.
3 You can't _____ a _____ if you don't bring the receipt with you.
4 My brother works as a _____ in a sports shop. He really enjoys it.
5 Some people prefer _____, but I'd rather visit real shops.
6 When I go shopping, I don't buy _____. They're expensive!

3 💡 **Read the *I'm learning* box. Read and complete the sentences with shopping and money verbs.**

> **I'm learning**
>
> **Shopping and money verbs**
> There are some verbs that we often use when we talk about shopping and money.
> Shops **sell** things to customers.
> Customers **buy** things from shops.
> You can **save** money for later.
> You can **spend** money in shops.

1 I don't usually ___spend___ a lot of money on clothes.
2 My rucksack is quite old. I need to _____ a new one.
3 They _____ some really nice clothes in that shop.
4 I don't have enough money for a comic. I need to _____ some money.
5 We don't have any milk, so we need to _____ some later.
6 How much money do you _____ on sweets each week?
7 My parents are trying to _____ money so we can all go on holiday this year.

4 💡 **Write five or more sentences using the shopping and money verbs from Activity 3.**

WOW! Team Talk 6

1 (6.4) **Read and complete the sentences from the dialogue on Pupil's Book page 74. Then listen and check.**

1 No _____chance_____ ! I don't like shopping.

2 I _____! I'm only kidding!

3 It's just such a waste of _____.

4 But _____ about clothes and shoes?

5 What do you do if they aren't big _____?

6 Hmm. I _____ so.

7 You don't get that _____.

8 If that happens, I won't be _____.

2 **Read the dialogue again. Circle T (true) or F (false). Then explain your answers.**

1 Mateo says he wants to go shopping. **T / (F)**
_He says he doesn't like shopping.___

2 Mei has already seen Mateo's blog. **T / F**
_____

3 Mateo's parents don't buy things online. **T / F**
_____

4 Mei says she doesn't like going to shops. **T / F**
_____

5 Mateo says he doesn't have to wait online. **T / F**
_____

6 Mei won't be sad if all the shops close. **T / F**
_____

3 (6.5) **Read and complete the dialogues with the correct expressions. Then listen and check.**

(No chance!) x 2   (I'm only kidding!) x 2   (That's true.) x 2

1 **A:** Don't buy that bag. You don't need it.
   B: ____That's true.____ I have lots of bags.
   A: You can buy it for me, if you like!

2 **A:** Do you want a burger for lunch?
   B: Of course not! I don't eat meat.
   A: _____ We're having salad.

3 **A:** Let's go to the cinema this evening.
   B: _____ I have to study for tomorrow's Maths test.
   A: OK. Let's go at the weekend then.

4 **A:** I got 40 pounds for my birthday.
   B: You should probably save some of it.
   A: _____ I might need it later.

5 **A:** Can my friends come over, Mum?
   B: _____ I've just cleaned the house.
   A: That's OK. We'll play in the garden.

6 **A:** Oh, no! The Wi-Fi isn't working.
   B: What? We don't have internet?
   A: Ha ha. _____ Don't worry!

4 **Work in pairs. Write another dialogue for each expression. Then act out the dialogues.**

Grammar

Zero and first conditionals

1 🎧 **(6.8) Listen and circle the correct words.**

1 If she wants a book, she gets it from a …
   a bookshop (**b** library) **c** friend
2 If he returns the shirt, he will ask for a …
   a different colour **b** refund **c** bigger size
3 If there's a long queue she will …
   a complain **b** return later **c** wait
4 If he needs clothes, he buys them …
   a in small shops **b** second-hand **c** online

2 **Read and complete the zero conditional sentences.**

1 If Martina _____needs_____ (need) to buy something, she always _____looks_____ (look) for the best price.
2 I _____ (get) very angry if someone _____ (be) rude to me.
3 My parents _____ (not be) happy if I _____ (spend) too much money.
4 If you _____ (feel) hungry, you _____ (have) to take a break and eat.
5 If we _____ (go) to the shopping centre on Saturdays, we _____ (have) lunch there.
6 If Diego _____ (want) some new music, he _____ (buy) it online.

3 **Read and complete the sentences.**

a we'll bring the music.	**d** ~~I will celebrate.~~
b we won't be tired.	**e** I'll buy some shoes.
c I'll be quite angry.	**f** she won't be happy.

1 If I pass the Maths exam, _I will celebrate._
2 If we rest now, _____
3 If I don't help Amy, _____
4 If we go shopping, _____
5 If I lose my bag, _____
6 If you have a party, _____

4 💡 **Read and complete the first conditional questions. Then write the answers.**

1 What _____will you do_____ (you / do) if it rains this weekend?
2 If you go to the shopping centre tomorrow, where _____ (you / have) lunch?
3 When _____ (you / study) if you have an English test next Monday?
4 If you get some money for your next birthday, how _____ (you / spend) it?
5 What _____ (you / say) if someone invites you to a party next weekend?

5 💬 **Work with your partner. Ask and answer the questions from Activity 4. Write their answers in your notebook.**

》》 Grammar reference, page 123

1 **After you read** Read the poem on Pupil's Book page 76 again. Number the sentences in order.

a ☐ I'd walk on the Moon, I'd look down at Earth …

b ☐ If I could travel the world one day, …

c ☐ I'd like to become Sherlock Holmes, …

d ☐ 1 If I could travel back in time, …

e ☐ I'd go to the Arctic, I'd play in the ice …

f ☐ If I could go into space, …

g ☐ I'd go to Ancient Egypt to see the pyramids …

h ☐ If I could become a character, …

2 Answer the questions. Write complete sentences.

1 When did the speaker learn about the pyramids?   *The speaker learned about them in History last year.*

2 How did the speaker dress up at school? _____

3 Why does the speaker say Sherlock is clever? _____

4 Who were the first people on the Moon? _____

5 What did the astronauts leave on the Moon? _____

6 Why must the speaker visit the Arctic soon? _____

3 Read the *Work with words* box. Write the correct prepositions.

Work with words

Collocations: *look* + preposition

We can make collocations with prepositions after the verb *look*.

*The teacher told us to **look at** the board.*

1   2   3   4   5   6

___up___   _____   _____   _____   _____

4 Read and complete the sentences with collocations with *look* from Activity 3.

1 Look ____*behind*____ you! Is there someone following you?

2 Don't look _____ at the Sun or you could hurt your eyes.

3 I looked _____ the room, but I couldn't see my bag.

4 Nadia found her phone when she looked _____ the table.

5 We can't look _____ the window because it's dirty.

6 Mehdi climbed the mountain and looked _____ at the ocean.

5 💡 Write six sentences with the collocations with *look* from Activity 4.

Vocabulary and Grammar

1 🎧 **6.12 Listen and complete the sentences.**

1 My brother would like to become an astronaut one day and ___go into space___ .

2 I'd like to _____ in the future, but I don't want to work!

3 Most students have to _____ if they want to finish school.

4 Would you like to _____ alone or would you prefer to go with a friend?

5 You might _____ if you visit Hollywood, in California.

6 Our school team could _____ this year if they practise a lot.

2 **Read and complete the questions.**

> a film character   travel back in time   be invisible
> become the leader   to a charity   three wishes

1 Would it be fun to ___be invisible___ so that no one else could see you?

2 Would you like to _____ of your country when you're older?

3 Would you like to donate _____ that helps other people?

4 Would you like to work in Hollywood and become _____ ?

5 Would you like to have _____ so that you can stop global warming?

6 Would you like to _____ to visit Ancient Egypt?

3 💬 **Work with your partner. Ask and answer the questions in Activity 2. Do you have similar answers?**

Second conditional

4 **Read and complete the sentences. Use the second conditional.**

1 I can't see the snake. I'm not scared.
  If I could see the snake, _I would be scared._

2 I don't know the answer. I won't tell you.
  If I knew the answer, _____

3 We don't have time. We won't visit the museum
  If we had the time, _____

4 I don't speak Italian. I don't understand Mario
  If I spoke Italian, _____

5 Ximena isn't here. She won't see the film.
  If Ximena was here, _____

6 You aren't 17. You can't drive a car.
  If you were 17, _____

5 **Read and complete the questions. Use the second conditional.**

IMAGINE THIS!

1 If you ___got___ (get) £100 for your birthday, what ___would you buy___ (you / buy)?

2 If you _____ (have) two weeks holidays now, where _____ (you / go)?

3 If you _____ (can) choose anywhere in the world, where _____ (you / live)?

4 If you _____ (meet) your favourite celebrity, what _____ (you / say)?

5 If you _____ (lose) your mobile phone, how _____ (you / feel)?

6 If you _____ (can) become anyone in the world, who _____ (you / choose)?

6 💡 **Write five more questions using your own ideas. Then ask and answer with your partner.**

>> Grammar reference, page 123

1   **After you read**   **Read the text on Pupil's Book page 78 again. What do the sentences describe? Write.**

1   You can see fun shows with animals.   *Djemaa el Fna* _____

2   The market isn't located on land. It's on a river.   _____

3   The things that you can buy there smell amazing.   _____

4   It's a great place to buy not very expensive gifts.   _____

5   It's famous for bags, shoes and other leather items.   _____

6   The market starts at 7 o'clock in the morning.   _____

2   **Answer the questions. Write complete sentences.**

1   Which time does the Hong Kong Flower Market close?

   The Hong Kong Flower Market closes at 7 pm.

2   How often is there a market in Djemaa el Fna?

   _____

3   What time must you go to the Muara Kuin Market?

   _____

4   How big did the Chiang Mai Night Bazaar use to be?

   _____

5   Which market should you visit if you want to buy a tree?

   _____

3   (6.14) **Listen to a report about another market. Complete the text.**

The Grand Bazaar is a ¹ _*famous*_ market. It's in Istanbul, which is the biggest city in Turkey. It's an indoor market and it's ² _____. It has about 60 different ³ _____ and more than 3,000 shops. You can buy so many different things there, for example, food, ⁴ _____ and carpets. The Grand Bazaar first opened in ⁵ _____ and now more than 250,000 people go there every day! Tourists often visit the market to ⁶ _____ traditional souvenirs, but you can also find many ⁷ _____ items. And if you want to take a break or get ⁸ _____, there are many cafés and restaurants.

4   **Work in groups. Choose one of the markets in the box and find answers to the questions. Write about your market.**

> Rialto Market (Venice, Italy)   St. Lawrence Market (Toronto, Canada)
> Queen Victoria Market (Melbourne, Australia)   Borough Market (London, England)

1   Where is the market?   4   What items do the shops sell?

2   How big is the market?   5   How many people go there?

3   What time is the market open?   6   What is special about the market?

English in action
Making a complaint

1 (6.17) **Read and complete the dialogue. Then listen and check.**

> **a** No, it fits, but there is a button missing.
> **b** Let me see. Oh, yes. Here you go.
> **c** No, thanks. Please could I have a refund?
> **d** They're damaged here. I need to exchange them.
> **e** I'm afraid I have a complaint about these jeans.
> **f** I'm afraid there's a problem with this jacket, too.

Adam: ¹ _e I'm afraid I have a complaint about these jeans._

Shop assistant: Oh, really? What's seems to be wrong with them?

Adam: ² _____

Shop assistant: I'm sorry about that. Of course you can exchange them.

Adam: ³ _____

Shop assistant: What's the problem? Is it too big or too small for you?

Adam: ⁴ _____

Shop assistant: Oh, I'm sorry about that. Do you want to exchange it?

Adam: ⁵ _____

Shop assistant: Yes, of course, I'll just need to see your receipt.

Adam: ⁶ _____

Shop assistant: That's great, thanks.

2 ✳ **Read and complete the dialogues with your own ideas. Then act out with your partner.**

1 A: I'd like to complain about this

_____ .

B: Oh, really? What's wrong with it?

A: _____ .

2 A: I'm afraid there's a problem with these

_____ .

B: What's the problem? Are they too big or too small?

A: _____ .

3 A: Excuse me. I need to exchange this

_____ .

B: Of course. What's the problem with it?

A: _____ .

Pronunciation

3 (6.18) 💬 **Listen and complete the second conditional sentences. Use 'd or would and a verb from the box. Then practise with your partner.**

> become   go   take   ~~buy~~   choose   make

1 If I won 1,000 pounds in a competition,
I ___would buy___ myself a new bike.

2 If I could have any job in the world,
I _____ a pilot.

3 If I were the President of our country,
I _____ a lot of changes.

4 If I had a big house near the beach,
I _____ there every weekend.

5 If I could learn to play any instrument,
I _____ the electric guitar.

6 If I met my favourite Hollywood actor,
I _____ a selfie, of course!

Words in context

1 **Read the definitions and write the words.**

enormous   embarrassed   incredible   jealous   underwater

1   When something is under the surface of water.   *underwater*

2   This is when you are unhappy that someone has something you
don't have.   _____

3   This is anything that seems extremely large in size or quantity.   _____

4   This is when you feel very shy or uncomfortable.   _____

5   This is something that is very difficult or impossible to believe.   _____

2 **Read the emails on Pupil's Book page 80 again. Read and complete the sentences.**
Who wrote them? Write *Tessa* or *Sam*.

1   *Sam*   If you have _____ *time* _____ , look at the _____ *website* _____ . I know you'll love it!

2   _____   I _____ the problem to the shop _____ .

3   _____   If you get _____ of shopping, you can visit the _____ .

4   _____   I felt so _____ ! I got out of the shop as _____ as I could.

5   _____   If I _____ , I would get on a _____ and come right now!

6   _____   I had to _____ and tell you about the _____ centre that we visited.

3 **Read the sentences and circle *T* (true) or *F* (false). Then explain your answers.**

1   Tessa was enjoying a holiday
in Dubai.   T / (F)

   Sam was enjoying a holiday in Dubai.

2   Sam had never seen such a big shopping
centre before.   T / F

_____

3   There wasn't anywhere to eat in the
shopping centre.   T / F

_____

4   Tessa wrote that she wasn't enjoying
herself at home.   T / F

_____

5   Tessa wanted to exchange the
T-shirt for a different colour.   T / F

_____

6   The T-shirt was small because
it didn't belong to Tessa.   T / F

_____

4 **Work in groups. Choose one of the shopping centres in the box. Discuss the**
questions and make notes. Then share your ideas with the class.

The West Edmonton Mall (Canada)   The Mall of America (USA)
Forum Istanbul (Turkey)   Galerías Pacífico (Argentina)

1   Where is the shopping centre?
2   How many shops does it have?
3   What fun activities can you do there?

4   Where can you go for something to eat?
5   What makes it special or unusual?

Literacy: emails

Writing

1 **Rewrite the sentences with *unless*.**

1 If I don't go to bed early, I'll feel tired tomorrow.

Unless I go to bed early, I'll feel tired tomorrow.

2 We'll miss the last bus if we don't leave now.

_____

3 If Emilia doesn't call me today, I'll be angry with her.

_____

4 You won't get a refund if you don't have a receipt.

_____

5 If the shop doesn't open soon, I'll have to leave.

_____

> **tip** **Writing**
>
> *unless*
> We use the word *unless* for
> *if … not.*
> *I won't have time to get it*
> ***unless I go*** *this weekend.* =
> ***if I don't go*** *this weekend.*

2 Imagine you've just visited the shopping centre you made notes on in Lesson 8. **Plan an email to a friend at home.**

Explain why you are sending an email.

Start with *Dear* or *Hi* and your friend's name.

Use paragraphs to organise your ideas clearly.

Use very clear, simple, everyday language.

Finish your email with *Bye* or *See you soon* and your name.

3 **Now write your email.**

4 **Check your work. Tick (✓) the steps when you have done them.**

Have I organised my email so it's easy to understand clearly? ☐

Have I used conditional sentences correctly? ☐

Have I used clear and simple language? ☐

Have I used the correct words to start and end the email? ☐

1 **Look at the picture and write the words.**

1 _____receipt_____
2 _____
3 _____
4 _____
5 _____
6 _____

2 **Read and complete the sentences with phrases.**

1 I'd like to _____travel back in time_____ to the 1900s.

2 Would you like to _____ and see every country on Earth?

3 I'd like to _____ – maybe a singer like Taylor Swift.

4 I'd like to _____ then I could buy nice things for my friends and family.

5 Would you like to _____? Then you could do any job you wanted!

3 **Read and complete the zero and first conditional sentences with your own ideas.**

1 If I don't have any breakfast, I always _____

2 If I don't finish my project today, _____

3 If the weather isn't nice, we usually _____

4 If we go shopping this weekend, _____

5 If my parents order pizza tonight, _____

4 **Read and write second conditional sentences.**

1 I'm not rich.
   If I were rich, I'd buy a big house.

2 Today isn't Friday.
   _____

3 We don't live in London.
   _____

4 You aren't British.
   _____

5 I can't fly.
   _____

6 We aren't in space.
   _____

Self-evaluation

5 **Answer the questions about your work in Unit 6.**

1 How was your work in this unit? Choose. ☐ OK ☐ Good ☐ Excellent

2 Which lesson was your favourite? _____

3 Which parts of the unit were difficult for you? _____

4 What new things can you talk about now? _____

5 How can you work and learn better in the next unit? _____

B1 Preliminary for Schools Listening Part 1

 1 Read the task carefully. Make sure you know what you have to do.

 2 🎧6.21 **How much does the jacket cost? Listen and choose the correct picture. Then explain your answer.**

A ☐   B ☐   C ☐

Do! **3** 🎯 🎧6.22 **Listen. For each question, choose the correct picture.**

> **tip** Exam
>
> Use the second listening to check your answer is correct, focusing on the key information in the text.

1 What is the special sale on T-shirts today?

A ☐   B ☐   C ☐

3 What time will the shop close this evening?

A ☐   B ☐   C ☐

2 Whose birthday is it on Saturday?

A ☐   B ☐   C ☐

4 What will Katy wear to the party?

A ☐   B ☐   C ☐

B1 Preliminary for Schools Writing Part 2

Think! 1 Read the task carefully. Make sure you know what you have to do.

Do! 2 🎯 Write an answer to one of the questions in the box below.

Question 1:
You see this notice on an international website. Write your article in about 100 words.

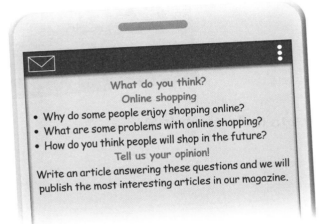

What do you think?
Online shopping
- Why do some people enjoy shopping online?
- What are some problems with online shopping?
- How do you think people will shop in the future?
Tell us your opinion!
Write an article answering these questions and we will publish the most interesting articles in our magazine.

tip Exam
Make sure you write the correct number of words and include all three elements of the message in your answer.

tip Exam
Make sure you write the correct number of words and your story continues from the sentence given.

Question 2:
Your English teacher asked you to write a story. Your story must begin with this sentence. Write your story in about 100 words.

I heard a noise in the kitchen and so I opened my bedroom door.

_____
_____
_____
_____
_____

check! 3 Check your work. Tick (✓) when you have completed the tasks for your question.

Question 1:
- ☐ I've written about 100 words.
- ☐ I've included all the parts of the notice in my article.
- ☐ My article is well-organised.
- ☐ I've used appropriate language and vocabulary.

Question 2:
- ☐ I've written about 100 words.
- ☐ My story continues nicely from the sentence given.
- ☐ My story is well-organised.
- ☐ I've used appropriate language and vocabulary.

Mateo's Learning club

Language booster 2

1 **After you read** Read the text on Pupil's Book page 84 again. Write *True* or *False*.

1 The skin of polar bears is white. _____*False*_____

2 Male polar bears can weigh the same as ten men. _____

3 Polar bears sometimes eat fish. _____

4 Polar bears can only swim for a few hours. _____

5 The number of polar bears is going down. _____

2 Rewrite the false sentences from Activity 1 to make them true.

_____

_____

3 Write the numbers in words as we say them.

1 **103**

_____one hundred and three_____

2 **250**

_____

3 **580**

_____

4 **605**

_____

5 **950**

_____

6 **1,000**

_____

4 Research and write one more fun fact and one more sad fact about polar bears.

Fun fact 4: _____

_____

Sad fact 4: _____

_____

5 Read and listen to the dialogue on Pupil's Book page 85 again. Answer the questions.

1 What do John and Nadia want to do?

_____

2 How are they going to get other people to help?

_____

6 Write suggestions.

disappeared   improved   invented   ~~recycled~~   saved   wasted

1 Put the plastic in that box so it can be <u>used again</u>.   _____recycled_____

2 Large parts of sea ice in the Arctic have <u>gone away</u>.   _____

3 I <u>was the first person to think</u> of this game.   _____

4 We've <u>used too much</u> water this summer.   _____

5 We've <u>helped</u> lots of polar bears.   _____

6 Renewable energy has <u>got better</u> in the last few years.   _____

7 Read and circle.

1 You can't do this job by **myself** / **yourself**.

2 I want to travel around the world by **myself** / **yourself**.

3 I often walk to school by **myself** / **yourself**.

4 Did you do this project by **myself** / **yourself**?

5 I ate the whole pizza by **myself** / **yourself**!

6 I want to go shopping by **myself** / **yourself** today.

8 Research and write three more ideas for the 'Go Green Game'.

Let's talk!

Vocabulary

1 **Read and circle the correct options.**

1 I'm going to **insert** / **listen** / **use** to a podcast about technology.

2 Lisa likes to **chat** / **receive** / **get** to friends online in the evening.

3 My dad doesn't like **writing** / **using** / **seeing** social media.

4 We'd like to want to **watch** / **get** / **use** a vlog about life in the USA.

5 If I don't **get** / **have** / **keep** a promise, I usually feel bad about it.

6 Most people think that it's wrong to **tell** / **listen** / **receive** a lie.

2 💬 **Unscramble the survey questions. Then ask and answer with your partner.**

What are you like?

1 Do you _____*get on well*_____ egt no lelw with most people?

2 Do you often _____ ceevrie xett samsegse from your friends?

3 Could you _____ pkee a creste if your friend told you one?

4 Do you usually _____ ltle eth utthr to your friends?

5 How often do _____ rnsiet na jmeoi in messages?

6 Did you _____ veah na tngrumae with anyone yesterday?

3 💡 **Read the *I'm learning* box. Then match the pairs of opposites.**

> badly   keep   truth   send   ~~tell~~

I'm learning

Remembering opposites
Some verbs and expressions have opposites. We can learn them as pairs.
speak to me / *listen* to me

1 If you can't **keep** a secret, people won't _____*tell*_____ you any.

2 I don't get on **well** with Hassan. We usually get on _____.

3 There's no mobile phone signal, so I can't **receive** or _____ a text message.

4 You know you shouldn't tell **lies**, you should always tell the _____.

5 You should try to _____ a promise. You shouldn't **break** it.

4 💡 **Write five or more sentences about how you communicate with other people. Use expressions from this lesson and any other expressions you know.**

1 (7.4) **Read and complete the sentences from the dialogue on Pupil's Book page 90. Then listen and check.**

> angry   arguments   blogs   borrow   cool   easy
> experiences   huge   maybe   ~~month~~   podcasts   ~~trying~~

1 I'm ___*trying*___ to get on well with everyone for a ___*month*___ .

2 Well, it's been _____ with my friends. I haven't had any _____ with them.

3 I was so _____ and we had a _____ argument!

4 _____ you should record your _____ in some way.

5 I think that _____ will be as popular as _____ one day.

6 I think it's a _____ T-shirt! Just don't let my sister _____ it!

2 **Read the dialogue again and circle _T_ (true) or _F_ (false). Then explain your answers.**

1 Mateo has been doing an experiment for a week. **T** / **F**
He's been doing an experiment for a month.

2 Mateo gets on worse with his sister than with his friends. **T** / **F**
_____

3 Mateo ruined his sister's favourite T-shirt. **T** / **F**
_____

4 Sophia thinks Mateo's experiment was successful. **T** / **F**
_____

5 Mateo thinks that podcasts are better than vlogs. **T** / **F**
_____

6 Sophia says that she never listens to podcasts. **T** / **F**
_____

3 (7.5) **Read and complete the dialogues with the correct expressions. Then listen and check.**

(Never mind.) x 2   (That's not on.) x 2   (What are you up to?) x 2

1 A: Hi Amir. ¹ _What are you up to?_
B: Not much. I'm waiting for Ana, but she's late, as usual!
A: ² _____ She should try harder to be on time.
B: I know. It makes me so angry.
A: ³ _____ Let's chat until she arrives.
B: That's so nice of you!

2 A: Are you using my tablet without asking? ⁴ _____
B: I thought this was my tablet. They look the same! I'm really sorry.
A: ⁵ _____ We all make mistakes.
B: Thanks. ⁶ _____ Do you want to go for a walk?
A: That's a great idea.

4 **Work in pairs. Write another dialogue for each expression. Then act out the dialogues.**

Grammar

(not) as ... as

1 🎧 (7.8) **Listen and tick (✓) the correct sentences.**

Julie   Sarah

1 a Julie is as old as Sarah. ☐

  b Sarah isn't as old as Julie. ✓

2 a Julie swims as well as Sarah. ☐

  b Sarah doesn't swim as well as Julie. ☐

3 a Julie's hair is as dark as Sarah's. ☐

  b Sarah's hair isn't as fair as Julie's hair. ☐

4 a Julie isn't as tall as Sarah. ☐

  b Sarah is as tall as Julie. ☐

5 a Julie is as friendly as Sarah. ☐

  b Sarah isn't as friendly as Julie. ☐

6 a Julie isn't as funny as Sarah. ☐

  b Sarah is as shy as Julie. ☐

2 **Rewrite the sentences with (not) as ... as and the <u>underlined</u> adjective.**

1 Yusuf is <u>tall</u>, but Paul is much taller.

Yusuf ___*isn't as tall as*___ Paul.

2 You are 15 years <u>old</u>. Your friend is also 15.

You _____ your friend.

3 Lucia isn't a <u>tidy</u> person. Her sister is very tidy.

Lucia _____ her sister.

4 Jack and his brother are both <u>clever</u>.

Jack _____ his brother.

5 Beatriz is <u>creative</u>, but Rachel isn't.

Rachel _____ Beatriz.

6 You and I are both <u>confident</u> people.

I'm _____ you are.

3 **Look at the information. Write sentences with (not) as ... as.**

GABRIEL
- 12 years old
- 150 cm tall
- not keen on sports
- good at Maths
- very hard-working
- very bad at keeping secrets

NOAH
- 13 years old
- 150 cm tall
- very keen on sports
- not good at Maths
- very hard-working
- bad at keeping secrets

1 (old) Gabriel *isn't as old as Noah.*

2 (tall) Noah _____

3 (sports) Gabriel _____

4 (Maths) Noah _____

5 (hard-working) Gabriel _____

6 (bad) Noah _____

4 💡 **Think of two friends. Then write sentences to compare them. Use (not) as ... as.**

1 (old) ___*is/isn't as old as*___

2 (friendly) _____

3 (interested in pop music) _____

4 (good at languages) _____

5 (easy to get on with) _____

6 (confident) _____

5 💬 **Compare your sentences from Activity 4 with your partner.**

 Grammar reference, page 124

 Book Club

1 <u>After you read</u> **Read the playscript on Pupil's Book page 92 again. Who says the following lines? Write.**

1 _Paula_ Hang on a minute, guys.
2 _____ That really IS a crazy idea.
3 _____ That'll get us talking.
4 _____ I'll go first.
5 _____ You're 12 years old, aren't you?
6 _____ I want to have a go!
7 _____ Oh no! I did!
8 _____ Let's play another game.

2 **Answer the questions. Use complete sentences.**

1 Who noticed that no one was talking to each other?

Paula noticed that no one was talking
to each other.

2 What game did Paula suggest playing together?

_____

3 What mustn't the person in the middle say?

_____

4 How does Simon answer the first question?

_____

5 Who is the second person to sit in the middle?

_____

6 Why do they stop playing the game so quickly?

_____

3 **Read the _Work with words_ box. Then complete the table.**

Work with words

The suffix _-ment_

Some nouns are formed by adding the suffix _-ment_ to verbs.

embarrass → **embarrassment**

disappoint → **disappointment**

Verb	Noun
advertise	1 _advertisement_
2 _____	argument
disappoint	3 _____
4 _____	enjoyment
entertain	5 _____
6 _____	excitement
improve	7 _____
8 _____	movement

4 **Read and complete the sentences with the nouns from Activity 3.**

1 My brother and I had an _argument_ last night, but then we made up.
2 I could feel the _____ of the train as it was leaving the station.
3 There was a lot of _____ in the audience before the concert.
4 It was a big _____ when our team lost the championship.
5 There was a large _____ for blue jeans at the bus stop.
6 If you study hard, there will be an _____ in your exam results.
7 You could see the _____ on the children's faces. They loved the circus.
8 I don't think this is good _____. It really isn't very fun to watch.

5 💡 **Write five more sentences with the nouns from Activity 4.**

Vocabulary and Grammar

1 Read the clues and complete the crossword.

1 **M I S E R A B L E**

1 sad or unhappy
2 sad or angry
3 not funny or amusing
4 worried and not relaxed
5 quiet and very relaxed
6 pleased or happy

2 🎧 (7.12) Listen and circle the correct answers.

1 The boy is …
   a confused **b** curious **c** delighted
2 The girl sounds …
   a upset **b** miserable **c** proud
3 The boy sounds …
   a nervous **b** disappointed **c** calm
4 The girl sounds …
   a confused **b** disappointed **c** embarrassed
5 The boy sounds …
   a curious **b** upset **c** nervous
6 The girl sounds …
   a calm **b** jealous **c** amused

3 💬 Work with your partner. Talk about when you have felt these emotions in the past.

> confused delighted disappointed
> embarrassed nervous proud

Question tags

4 Read and complete the sentences with the correct question tags.

1 Camila doesn't like this music, ___*does she*___
2 This pizza is delicious, _____?
3 Speaking in front of the class makes you really nervous, _____?
4 Your friends aren't coming over for lunch tomorrow, _____?
5 Amanda isn't going to be late for school again today, _____?
6 You're doing your science project with Mehmet, _____?

5 Write the sentences with question tags

1 you / not / be / good at keeping secrets
   You aren't good at keeping secrets, are you?
2 you / often / use social media
   _____
3 you / have / never / break / a promise
   _____
4 you / like / stay / at home / at weekends
   _____
5 you / not / like / blogging
   _____
6 you / usually / be / a calm person
   _____

6 💡 Write five different sentences about your partner. Then say them to your partner using question tags. Were you right? Use the ideas in the box or your own ideas.

> • feel proud if pass your exams
> • know how to insert an emoji in an email
> • feel miserable if someone tells you a lie
> • don't get on well with lots of people
> • never tell the truth
> • don't like watching vlogs
> • feel calm when you go for a walk

》》 Grammar reference, page 124

1 **After you read** Read the text on Pupil's Book page 94 again. Then read and complete the sentences. Write one word in each gap.

1 We can ____communicate____ with each other ____without____ using any words.

2 Emojis are _____ that are used in social _____ and text messages.

3 Hieroglyphics are a _____ language that was used in _____ Egypt.

4 The _____ Day of Sign Languages is _____ on 23rd September.

2 Read the sentences and circle T (true) or F (false). Then explain your answers.

1 Some types of language use pictures instead of words.   (T)/ F

  Emojis and hieroglyphics use pictures.

2 Emojis aren't popular with 18–25 year-old people.   T / F

  _____

3 Sad emojis aren't used as often as happy emojis.   T / F

  _____

4 We can't understand what hieroglyphics mean.   T / F

  _____

5 There is more than one type of sign language.   T / F

  _____

3 (7.14) Listen to a report about another way of communicating without words. Complete the notes.

Language:
- Silbo Gomero
- a very unusual [1] ____whistling____ language
- now used by about [2] _____ people

Place used:
- used on the [3] _____ of La Gomera, which is part of Spain
- in the mountains, where people are separated by [4] _____
- easier than [5] _____ long distances to speak with people

History:
- used by the Guanches people for [6] _____ of years
- changed later to communicate the [7] _____ language
- became an official school subject on La Gomera in [8] _____
- recognised as a World Heritage language by UNESCO in [9] _____
- now popular with [10] _____ who come to La Gomera to hear it

4 Work in groups. Choose one of the ways of communicating from the box and find answers to the questions. Write about your way of communicating.

Semaphore   Morse code   Braille

1 Who invented this way of communicating?   3 How do people comunicate?

2 When was it invented?   4 Who uses this way of communicating?

English in action
Giving your opinion

1 (7.17) **Listen and order the phrases for giving opinions. Then listen again and complete.**

a ☐ Personally, I think that _____ .

b ☐ I bet that _____ .

c ☐ I'm certain that _____ .

d ☐ I'm sure that _____ .

e ☐ 1 I guess that _____ *he left it somewhere* _____ .

2 ✳ **Read and complete the dialogues with your own ideas. Then act out with your partner.**

1 Do you think it's OK to tell a lie to a good friend?

Personally, I think that _____ .

2 I saw Emily taking something out of your rucksack.

I'm certain that _____ .

3 Kevin is angry because you didn't talk to him at lunch.

I'm sure that _____ .

4 Sarah is disappointed because you broke a promise to her.

I guess that _____ .

5 I don't agree with your idea for our English project.

I bet that _____ .

Pronunciation

3 (7.18) 💬 **Listen and circle. Are the people checking that they're correct (C) or are they asking real questions (R)? Then practise with your partner.**

1 Marcus can't play the guitar, can he? ⓒ / R

2 You're good at keeping secrets, aren't you? C / R

3 Kate gets embarrassed easily, doesn't she? C / R

4 The students won't be nervous, will they? C / R

5 You get on quite well with Adam, don't you? C / R

6 You aren't worried about the exam, are you? C / R

Reading

Words in context

1 **Read and complete the definitions.**

age   interview   part   relationship   ~~shape~~

1 A sphere is an object that has a round _____*shape*_____ .
2 Your _____ is the number of years that have passed since you were born.
3 During a typical _____ , a person usually answers several questions.
4 I have a great _____ with my grandfather. We get on really well.
5 Physical exercise is an important _____ of a healthy lifestyle.

2 **Read the interview on Pupil's Book page 96 again. Match.**

1 Louise has written about
2 Oliver's friend shows him
3 Louise says we can make
4 We need to say that we
5 People may look happier
6 We may get jealous if we

a are sorry and try to forgive people.
b friends by being friendly and positive.
c in photographs than they really are.
d different friendships that people have.
e think other people's lives are better than ours.
f support and is proud of what he does.

3 **Answer the questions. Use complete sentences.**

1 When can people start buying Louise's book?
   People can start buying Louise's book next Monday.
2 When does Louise think friends are really important?
   _____
3 How much older than Oliver is his friend?
   _____
4 What can happen when you argue with a friend?
   _____
5 What things should you talk about with your friends?
   _____
6 Why don't people tell the truth on social media?
   _____

4 **Work in groups. Discuss the most important rules for a good friendship and make notes. Then share your ideas with the class. Have a class vote on the five best rules.**

Literacy: interviews

Writing

1 **Rewrite the sentences with _whereas._**

1 Samuel isn't friendly. His brother is very nice.

Samuel isn't friendly, whereas his brother is very nice.

2 My older brother is keen on social media. My parents never use it.

_____

3 Some people can keep promises. Other people break them.

_____

4 Ali made a vlog for his project. Leila did a podcast.

_____

5 I'm very calm before exams. My friends get really nervous.

_____

> **tip** **Writing**
>
> _whereas_
> _I'm chatty, energetic and bossy_
> **_whereas_** _she is quiet, calm and kind._
> We use _whereas_ to link two different things or ideas.

2 **Plan an interview about the things that are important for being a good student.**

Start by thanking the person for letting you interview them. →

Use clear, logical questions about your chosen topic. →

You can also use sentences with tag questions. →

Write the interview as a dialogue that's easy to read. →

Use language that is polite, but not too formal. →

Finish by thanking the person for answering your questions. →

3 **Now write your interview.**

4 **Check your work. Tick (✓) the steps when you have done them.**

Have I asked clear and interesting questions? ☐

Have I used language that is polite, but not too formal? ☐

Have I used language that is easy to read? ☐

Have I thanked the person? ☐

1 **Look and complete.**

 1  2  3  4  5  6

listen					
to a podcast	an emoji	a vlog	a text message	a secret	an argument

2 **Read and complete the sentences.**

confused   curious   delighted   ~~disappointed~~   jealous   miserable

1 If your favourite team loses a game, you may feel _____*disappointed*_____ .

2 If you want to learn something interesting, you are _____ about it.

3 When you don't understand something, you can get _____ easily.

4 If you win a prize or an award you will probably feel _____ about it.

5 If you receive some terrible news, you may feel _____ for a while.

6 When someone has something that you want, you may feel _____ .

3 **Read and write sentences with (not) as … as.**

1 Tom is friendly. Amy is friendlier.   Tom *isn't as friendly as Amy.* _____

2 Juan and Miguel are both 160 cm tall.   Miguel _____

3 New York is bigger than Chicago.   Chicago _____

4 You and I feel nervous.   I _____

5 Vicky's better at Science than Fatma.   Fatma _____

4 **Read and complete the sentences with the correct question tags.**

aren't you   does she   don't they   haven't we   ~~is he~~   will you

1 Emir's not here, _____*is he*_____ ?

2 You're good at Maths, _____ ?

3 They like pizza, _____ ?

4 You won't be late, _____ ?

5 We've finished, _____ ?

6 Emma doesn't ski, _____ ?

Self-evaluation

5 **Answer the questions about your work in Unit 7.**

1 How was your work in this unit? Choose. ☐ OK ☐ Good ☐ Excellent

2 Which lesson was your favourite? _____

3 Which parts of the unit were difficult for you? _____

4 What new things can you talk about now? _____

5 How can you work and learn better in the next unit? _____

Get ready for...

B1 Preliminary for Schools Listening Part 2

 1 Read the task carefully. Make sure you know what you have to do.

 2 Listen and choose the sentence with a similar meaning.

1 A Helen doesn't use social media very much now.

B Helen has stopped using social media during the day.

C Helen likes to watch vlogs about social media habits.

2 A George has just had a big argument with his friend Frank.

B George isn't happy because his friend Frank can't keep a secret.

C George and Frank aren't getting on because Frank doesn't always tell the truth.

Do! **3**   Listen. For each question, choose the correct answer.

1 You will hear a girl, Emma, talking to her friend, Michael. What does she want him to do this afternoon?

A go jogging with her

B listen to her science podcast

C keep his promise to help her

2 You will hear a boy, Oliver, doing a presentation. Why did he choose this topic?

A He read some articles online about it.

B He gets nervous and upset quite easily.

C He wanted to interview some people.

3 You will hear a teacher, Mrs Martin, talking to her class. How does she feel right now?

A She's delighted that everyone passed the test.

B She's upset that some people did poorly.

C She's proud of everyone whether or not they passed the test.

4 You will hear a brother and a sister, David and Sarah, talking. How does David feel?

A disappointed because he doesn't want pizza again

B delighted because he loves salad

C confused because he can't find the recipe

tip Exam

During the second listening, make sure you check all your answers carefully, focusing on specific information.

B1 Preliminary for Schools Reading Part 5

 1 **Read the task carefully. Make sure you know what you have to do.**

 2 **Read the sentences and choose the correct words.**

1 My brother talks too much and he's really bad at ... secrets.

   A staying   **B** keeping   **C** having   **D** making

2 Ariana got really ... when she fell off her bike and all her friends were watching.

   A miserable   **B** curious   **C** embarrassed   **D** serious

Do! **3** **Read the text below and choose the correct word for each space. For each question, mark the letter next to the correct word, A, B, C or D.**

tip Exam

Read the sentences carefully. What type of word is missing? Choose the best answer and then check the other three options and decide why they are wrong.

Internet anonymity

Have you ever received a nasty comment from **(1)** ... on social media which made you feel upset? Was it a person using their real name and photo or was it someone whose real identity was a **(2)** ...? This is what we call 'internet anonymity' and some experts think this is a **(3)** ... problem because it lets us write horrible things online without any consequences. After all, most people **(4)** ... never speak like that in a face-to-face conversation.

On the other hand, there are some benefits to online anonymity. People can give more honest opinions; they can tell the **(5)** ... about what they think and feel because they needn't worry about what other people will think. They can also criticise important people or **(6)** ... about the company where they work. In addition, people feel more comfortable writing about embarrassing problems when they are anonymous. What do you think?

1 A no one   **C** nobody
  B something   **D** someone

2 A lie   **C** truth
  B secret   **D** promise

3 A miserable   **C** serious
  B pround   **D** nervous

4 A would   **C** may
  B can   **D** don't

5 A promise   **C** secret
  B truth   **D** lie

6 A explain   **C** listen
  B suggest   **D** complain

Inventions

Vocabulary

1 **Label the inventions.**

1
It's an _X-ray_____.

2
It's a _____.

3
It's an _____.

4
It's a _____.

5
It's a _____.

6
It's a _____.

2 **Read and complete the sentences with inventions.**

1 A _____vaccination_____ can stop babies from getting sick.

2 The Apollo _____ took astronauts to the Moon.

3 Your TV uses _____ to produce sound and light.

4 The first trains had a _____ to make them go.

5 I need a better camera to do _____ as a hobby.

6 If you get sick, a doctor may give you _____ to help you feel better.

3 Read the *I'm learning* box. Use a dictionary to check the stress of the words. Then <u>underline</u> the stressed syllables.

> **I'm learning**
>
> **Checking the stress of words**
> When we learn new words, it's important to know how they are stressed. We can check the stress with a dictionary.
> <u>ra</u>dio   pho<u>tog</u>raphy   antibi<u>o</u>tics

1 <u>bat</u>tery

2 internet

3 vaccination

4 thermometer

5 engine

6 microwave

7 electricity

8 compass

9 aeroplane

10 spacecraft

4 Choose five or more words that you learned in other units and underline their stress. Then write a sentence using each of these words.

1 (8.4) **Match the two halves of the sentences from the dialogue on Pupil's Book page 102. Then listen and check.**

1 This is the room where

2 That's the radio which

3 She remembers the time

4 It was named after

5 They were the people who

a the person who invented it.

b my great-grandmother told me about.

c when everyone used radios like this.

d you can see lots of old inventions.

e invented the aeroplane, of course!

2 **Read the dialogue again. Choose *T* (true) or *F* (false). Then explain your answers.**

1 The radio in the museum was made in 1909. **T / (F)**

   The radio was made in 1904.

2 You push a button to turn on the Marconi radio. **T / F**

3 Two brothers won the Nobel Prize in 1909. **T / F**

4 Mateo says he's never seen a light bulb. **T / F**

5 Thomas Edison wasn't born in Italy in 1879. **T / F**

3 (8.5) **Read and complete the dialogues with the correct expressions. Then listen and check.**

(You're right!) × 2   (I'm not surprised.) × 2   (Nor have I,) × 2

1 **A:** Mum, I can't find my History book.
   B: Perhaps you left it in the dining room.
   A: *You're right!* Thanks, Mum.

2 **A:** Is the Science Museum open today?
   B: I don't know. I've never been there.
   A: _____ but I'd like to go.

3 **A:** Who won the Maths competition?
   B: It was Amira. She always wins.
   A: _____ She's so clever.

4 **A:** I haven't watched that new sci-fi film yet.
   B: _____ but it looks good.
   A: Let's watch it this evening.

5 **A:** Wow! That jacket's expensive!
   B: _____ It's a designer label.
   A: I suppose so, but that's a lot of money.

6 **A:** We should play outside today.
   B: _____ It's nice and sunny.
   A: But it's cold, so put on a jacket.

4 **Work in pairs. Write another dialogue for each expression. Then act out the dialogues.**

Grammar

Relative pronouns

1 🎧 **(8.8) Listen. Then circle T (true) or F (false).**

1 The person whose invention made ice cream more popular was from the UK.　**T / F**

2 The name of the person who invented the first ice cream maker was Nancy Johnson.　**T / F**

3 The year when this new machine was invented was 1943.　**T / F**

4 The machine was invented at a time when ice cream was quite expensive.　**T / F**

5 The only place where people could enjoy this new ice cream was in shops.　**T / F**

6 The new ice cream maker was a machine that used electricity.　**T / F**

2 **Read and complete the sentences with the correct relative pronouns.**

| that　when　where　~~which~~　who　whose |

1 Antibiotics are medicines _____*which*_____ can save lives.

2 A science museum is a place _____ you can learn about technology.

3 The Wright Brothers were the people _____ invented the first aeroplane.

4 The steam engine was an invention _____ changed history.

5 Bill Gates is a famous inventor _____ name everyone knows.

6 Your birthday is a special day _____ people buy you presents.

3 **Rewrite the sentences with relative pronouns.**

1 A phonograph is a machine. It records sound.

　A phonograph is a machine that records sound.

2 A lab is a place. We do experiments in a lab.

_____

3 Marconi was a scientist. He invented the radio.

_____

4 Electricity is a type of energy. We use it every day.

_____

5 Alfred Nobel was a man. His name is now famous.

_____

6 Summer is a season. We go to the beach.

_____

4 💡 **Write sentences with relative pronouns.**

1 I have a friend whose _*name is Rani*_.

2 The best day in my life was when _____

_____.

3 A hero is a person who _____

_____.

4 An great film is one which _____

_____.

5 I want to live in a place where _____

_____.

6 My favourite object is something that ___

_____.

5 💬 **Compare your sentences from Activity 4 with your partner.**

》》 Grammar reference, page 125

1 **After you read** **Read the story on Pupil's Book page 104 again. Number the sentences in order.**

- **a** The teacher asked Marina to do a presentation about Penicillin.
- **b** Marina told her class why she thought Dorothy's invention was important.
- 1 **c** Marina's mum took her to see the doctor.
- **d** The teacher said she hoped the class would invent things in the future.
- **e** Marina stood up and told her class all about Penicillin.
- **f** Marina's teacher told her what she knew about the medicine.
- **g** Marina was curious about Penicillin.
- **h** Marina told her class who Dorothy Hodgkin was.

2 **Answer the questions. Use complete sentences.**

1 When did Marina start to feel better?

She started to feel better after she had

taken some medicine.

2 How did Marina find out about Penicillin?

_____

3 Why did the doctor take Marina's temperature?

_____

4 Who felt relaxed during Marina's presentation?

_____

5 What type of laboratory did Dorothy Hodgkin work in?

_____

6 Where did Dorothy Hodgkin study and work?

_____

3 **Read the *Work with words* box. Then write the collocations with *take*.**

> **Work with words**
>
> **Collocations with *take***
>
> We can make collocations with *take* and various other words.
>
> Did you **take your medicine** today?
>
> Don't hurry. **Take your time**.

1 *take a pill*

2 _____

3 _____

4 _____

5 _____

6 _____

4 **Read and complete the sentences with the collocations with *take* from Activity 3.**

1 Are you feeling ill? Let me _____*take your temperature*_____.

2 I want to _____ and put it on my blog.

3 Oh! _____ at this dress! It's beautiful!

4 If you're tired, you can _____ and rest.

5 The doctor said to _____ every eight hours.

6 We can _____ of the museum tomorrow.

5 **Write six new sentences with the collocations with *take* from Activity 4.**

Vocabulary and Grammar

1 🎧 **8.12 Read and complete. Then listen and check.**

> carry out an experiment
> do some research   feel better   feel ill
> make a discovery   win a Nobel Prize

1 comment

Alice   1 day ago

I'd like to become a scientist when I'm older. I want to ¹ *do some research* to help other people who have an illness. I don't like it when I ² _____. My big dream is to ³ _____ to test a new medicine. If I ⁴ _____, I might become world famous. And if my work makes lots of people ⁵ _____, I might also ⁶ _____! That would be amazing!

2 🎧 **8.13 Listen and circle T (true) or F (false).**

1 a Sarah says she has a fever today.   **T / F**

   b Dad says she'll feel better after a rest.   **T /(F)**

2 a The boy didn't need to have an injection.   **T / F**

   b He's going to get a prescription later.   **T / F**

3 a Emma had an operation on her foot.   **T / F**

   b She might need to have an X-ray.   **T / F**

3 💬 **Talk about your health experiences with your partner.**

> Have you ever had an operation?

> No, I haven't.

Embedded questions

4 **Read the questions about the Science Museum. Then complete the embedded questions.**

At the Science Museum

1 When does the museum open?
2 Is there a special price for students?
3 Can we take photos?
4 Are there any old inventions?
5 Where we can have a snack?
6 Is the museum open on Mondays?

1 Can you tell us   *when the museum opens*

2 Do you know whether _____

3 I wonder if _____

4 Could you tell me if _____

5 Do you know if _____

6 I wonder whether _____

5 **Read the answers. Then write embedded questions.**

1 **A:** Can you tell us   *where the museum shop is* ?

   B: Yes, the museum shop is over there.

2 **A:** Do you know if _____ ?

   B: No, there isn't a pharmacy near here.

3 **A:** Could you tell me _____ ?

   B: Yes, it's half past seven.

4 **A:** I wonder whether _____ ?

   B: No, we shouldn't go out now.

5 **A:** Can you tell me _____ ?

   B: Yes, I'm fifteen years old.

6 💬 **Write five questions for your partner. Then take turns saying your questions and changing them to embedded questions.**

>>> Grammar reference, page 125

1 **After you read** Read the text on Pupil's Book page 106 again. Read and complete the sentences with the correct words.

1 David Cohen designed a robot to help people _A_ were trapped underground.

  A who   **B** which   **C** when

2 David got the idea for his new invention ___ learning about worms at school.

  A before   **B** where   **C** after

3 Anurudh Ganesan invented a special bicycle ___ could keep vaccinations cool.

  A it   **B** that   **C** what

4 Anurudh's new bicycle works without ___ electricity or ice.

  A using   **B** use   **C** used

5 Thato Kgatlhanye's bags store solar energy, ___ they don't need electricity.

  A why   **B** which   **C** so

6 The new school bags produce light so that children ___ study at home.

  A must   **B** can   **C** don't

2 Answer the questions. Write complete sentences.

1 How old was David when he designed his robot?

  David was thirteen years old when he designed his robot.

2 What is special about the way that David's robot moves?

  _____

3 Who did Anurudh want to help with his invention?

  _____

4 What part of the bike keeps the vaccinations cool?

  _____

5 What materials are used to make Thato's school bags?

  _____

  _____

6 Why should children carry brightly-coloured bags?

  _____

3 (8.15) Listen to a report about another invention. Complete the text.

Banana plastic!

Elif Bilgin from Turkey, was only 16 years old when she ¹____won____ the Science in Action Award for an ²_____ invention. She discovered a way to ³_____ banana peel – the part we don't eat – and make it into a ⁴_____ type of plastic. Elif carried out ⁵_____ for two years until she made her big ⁶_____ – a plastic that was strong and ⁷_____ enough to make medical equipment. Elif thinks her plastic could replace petrol in ⁸_____. That would ⁹_____ keep the air and the environment ¹⁰_____.

4 Work in groups. Choose one of the inventors in the box and find answers to the questions. Write about your inventor.

Alexander Graham Bell (telephone) John Logie Baird (television)
Josephine Cochrane (dishwasher) Percy Spencer (microwave)

1 Where was the inventor from?
2 How did he/she become an inventor?
3 What is the invention and what is it used for?
4 When did he/she make the invention?
5 Why did people need the invention?
6 How quickly did it become popular?

English in action
Talking about how sure you are

1 (8.18) **Read and complete the dialogue. Then listen and check.**

a Lots of things use batteries today	**e** Edison invented the electric light bulb
b Those inventions use batteries today	**f** That's why Edison is the best inventor
c I think his work was more important	**g** Volta invented the first battery
d I think that Alessandro Volta	**h** But what other things did he invent

Lisa: ¹ _____d I think that Alessandro Volta_____ was the greatest inventor of all time.

Paul: Do you really think that? I know that ² _____, but other people have done more.

Lisa: Yes, I'm quite sure. ³ _____.

Paul: Maybe, but what about Thomas Edison? ⁴ _____.

Lisa: Oh, come on! Are you sure about that?

Paul: Yes! I'm absolutely sure! ⁵ _____.

Lisa: Yes, I know that. ⁶ _____?

Paul: He invented a phonograph to record music and he invented the movie camera. ⁷ _____.

Lisa: Hmm, I doubt it. ⁸ _____!

2 (8.19) ✴ **Listen and complete the dialogues. Then act them out with your partner.**

1 A: In the future, I think people will go to the Moon on holiday.

B: No way! ¹ _____Do you really think that_____?

A: Oh, yes. ² _____.
What do you think?

B: ³ _____. Space travel is too expensive.

2 A: Do you think there will be paper books in the future?

B: ⁴ _____, but most people will read books on tablets.

A: Really? ⁵ _____?

B: ⁶ _____. Paper books are old-fashioned.

Pronunciation

3 (8.20) 💬 **Read and complete the sentences. Listen and repeat. Then practise with a partner.**

that when where ~~which~~ who

1 Batteries are things _____which_____ many machines use today.

2 Marconi was the scientist _____ invented the radio.

3 The 20ᵗʰ century was a time _____ many things were invented.

4 The phonograph was a machine _____ recorded sounds.

5 Kitty Hawk is the town _____ the Wright Brothers flew their aeroplane.

Reading

Words in context

1 **Read and complete the sentences.**

blackboard   generations   items   list   ~~rows~~   time capsule

1 There are four _____*rows*_____ of desks in my class and I sit next to my best friend, Bella.

2 In the past, teachers wrote on a _____. Now they use a whiteboard.

3 When my grandfather was a boy he found a _____ buried in his garden.

4 You can make a _____ of things you need to pack before you go on holiday.

5 We must protect the rainforests for future _____ to enjoy.

6 I found this box in our attic. It has some really interesting _____ in it.

2 **Read the letter on Pupil's Book page 108 again. Read and complete the sentences.**

1 But the most interesting ____*thing*____ was this old ____*letter*____ that I found.

2 _____ you're reading this, then you have _____ our time capsule!

3 She's the teacher _____ lessons we all _____!

4 In the _____, we sit in rows in _____ of Mrs Parks.

5 _____ Mrs Parks comes into the classroom, we _____ up.

6 In our _____, there are some _____ cars.

3 **Answer the questions. Use complete sentences.**

1 When did Marion and her friends put the time capsule in the wall?

They put the time capsule in the wall in 1953.

2 Where did Marion live when she wrote the letter?

_____

3 How old was Marion when she wrote the letter?

_____

4 Where did Mrs Parks write things in the classroom?

_____

5 What did Marion and her friends wear to school?

_____

6 How did people use to travel to London?

_____

4 **Work in groups. Imagine you're going to make a time capsule. Look at the ideas in the box and decide which items you would put in it or use your own ideas. Discuss and make notes. Then share your ideas with the class.**

classroom objects   technology
music   art   photos
a letter/postcard/email
clothes   food

Literacy: letters

Writing

1 **Rewrite the sentences with *as much as*.**

1 My grandmother likes baking cakes. I like eating them.

My grandmother likes baking cakes as much as I like eating them.

2 I enjoy buying clothes. My sister enjoys buying books.

_____

3 Elena goes cycling a lot. Feng goes running a lot.

_____

4 We like having parties. Other people like coming to them.

_____

5 I love dogs. You love cats.

_____

2 Imagine you're making a time capsule for your grandchildren. Plan a letter to include in the time capsule.

Include your address at the top right of the letter.

Put the date under your address.

Start the letter with *Dear grandchildren,*

Describe life in the world now.

Explain what's in your time capsule and why.

Finish the letter with *Love from* + your name.

3 **Now write your letter.**

4 **Check your work. Tick (✓) the steps when you have done them.**

Have I started and finished the letter correctly? ☐

Have I included my address? ☐

Have I described what's in my time capsule and why? ☐

Have I used *as much as* correctly? ☐

① Write the inventions. What's the mystery word?

	1									
1	A	N	T	I	B	I	O	T	I	C	S
2										
3										
4										
5										
6										

The mystery word is _____.

② Read and complete the sentences.

> carry out an experiment   do some research   feel better
> get a prescription   ~~have a fever~~   have an X-ray

1 My face looks red and I feel ill. I think I _____ *have a fever* _____.
2 I need to _____ on the internet for my Geography project.
3 Valentina can _____ for some medicine from her doctor.
4 My brother hurt his leg and he had to _____ to see if it was broken.
5 Mark's ill today, but I'm sure he'll _____ and be back at school tomorrow.
6 We're going to _____ in the Science laboratory at school.

③ Read and complete the sentences with relative pronouns.

1 The electric light bulb is an invention _____ *that* _____ changed the world.
2 Julia is the girl _____ Science project won first prize.
3 Autumn is the time of year _____ trees change colour.
4 The book _____ I lost on the bus belonged to Anna.
5 The first woman _____ won a Nobel Prize was Marie Curie.
6 I'd like to live in a city _____ there are lots of parks.

④ Write embedded questions.

1 Where's the Science lab?   Could you *tell me where the Science lab is?*
2 Is there a concert tonight?   I wonder _____
3 When does the next bus leave?   Can you _____
4 Is next Monday a holiday?   Do you know _____
5 Who is coming to visit us today? Could you _____

Self-evaluation

⑤ Answer the questions about your work in Unit 8.

1 How was your work in this unit? Choose.   ☐ OK   ☐ Good   ☐ Excellent
2 Which lesson was your favourite? _____
3 Which parts of the unit were difficult for you? _____
4 What new things can you talk about now? _____
5 How can you work and learn better in the next unit? _____

Get ready for...

Think! **1** Read the task carefully. Make sure you know what you have to do.

Try! **2** (8.23) Listen. For each question, choose the correct answer. Then explain your answers.

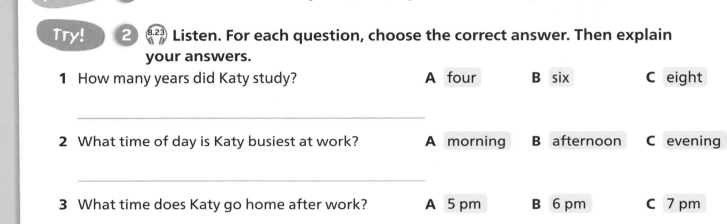

1 How many years did Katy study? **A** four **B** six **C** eight

_____

2 What time of day is Katy busiest at work? **A** morning **B** afternoon **C** evening

_____

3 What time does Katy go home after work? **A** 5 pm **B** 6 pm **C** 7 pm

_____

Do! **3** (8.24) For each question, write the correct answer in the gap. You will hear a woman called Holly Adams talking to a group of students about her work as a chemist. Write one or two words or a number or a date or a time.

My job as a chemist

Holly Adams works at a chemist's near the

(1) _____

She finished university in June **(2)** _____

Every day she prepares around **(3)** _____

medicine orders for her customers.

In the afternoon, she often reads articles about new

(4) _____

Once a month, Holly opens her chemist's on

(5) _____

The best part of her job is helping people who

(6) _____ about their health.

> **tip** **Exam**
>
> Use the order of the information on the page to help you follow the recording.

B1 Preliminary for Schools Writing Part 1

Think! **1** Read the task carefully. Make sure you know what you have to do.

Do! **2** You must answer this question. Write your answer in about 100 words. Read this email from your English-speaking friend Sophia, and the notes you have made.

send   forward   attach

To:

From: Sophia

Hi there,

Good news! I'm doing a presentation at the Inventor's Fair next Saturday and they gave me an extra ticket. Would you like to come? — **Excellent!**

My presentation is at 2 pm, but we can go earlier than that if you like. What time is best for you? — **Say what time**

There'll be other presentations on topics such as solar energy, recycling and robots. Which would you prefer to see? — **Tell Sophia**

After the fair, we can go somewhere for dinner.

Where would you like to go? — **Suggest**

See you soon,

Sophia

> **tip Exam**
> Make sure you read through your answer to ensure that everything you have written is clear and that you have included all the content points.

Write your email to Sophia, using all the notes.

check! **3** Check your work. Tick (✓) when you have completed the tasks for your question.

☐ I've written about 100 words.

☐ I've answered all of Sophia's questions.

☐ My email is well-organised.

☐ I've used appropriate language and vocabulary.

It's party time!

Vocabulary

1 Look and complete the crossword.

1 2 3

4 5 6

Crossword:

1 V I O L I N

2 Complete the comments on the music blog.

1 My dad loves _____*rock music*_____. His favourite band is the Rolling Stones.

2 Our school orchestra did a p_____ last week in the school hall.

3 Did you know j_____ combines African and American music?

4 I think o_____ is great. It combines singing with drama and costumes.

5 I'm from Ireland, where lots of people enjoy traditional f_____.

6 If I really like a film, I usually download the s_____ to my smartphone.

3 Read the *I'm learning* box. Then add four more examples to each set of words. Use a dictionary to help you.

I'm learning

Expanding sets of words
When we learn a set of words, we can expand it by adding more examples. We can use a dictionary to help.

Types of music
folk music, jazz music, rock music ...
pop music, classical music

Musical instruments

drums, flute, trumpet, violin,

Other music words

performance, soundtrack,

4 Write five or more sentences about musical instruments you play and music you enjoy. Use words from Activity 3.

1 🎧 9.5 **Read and complete the sentences from the dialogue on Pupil's Book page 114. Who said them? Write. Then listen and check.**

band   camera   day   ~~enjoy~~   excited   good   idea
keeps   keyboard   ~~makes~~   nervous   reminds

1 __Sophia__   I always ___enjoy___ watching the school concert. Music ___makes___ me feel happy!

2 _____   So do I! They were _____ this morning, but _____, too!

3 _____   He plays the _____, doesn't he? Who else is in his _____?

4 _____   They're really _____. They practise every _____ after school.

5 _____   Oh, that _____ me! I learned to use this _____ yesterday.

6 _____   ..., but my mum _____ saying that it isn't a good _____.

2 **Read the dialogue again and circle *T* (true) or *F* (false). Then explain your answers.**

1 Alex doesn't want to see the school performance.   **T** /Ⓕ   *Alex says that he can't wait for it.*

2 Mei is going to perform with the orchestra.   **T / F** _____

3 Sarah plays the drums in Mateo's band.   **T / F** _____

4 Alex is going to record the orchestra's performance.   **T / F** _____

5 Sophia says she wants to learn the drums.   **T / F** _____

6 Alex's mum doesn't want to hear loud music   **T / F** _____

3 🎧 9.6 **Read and complete the dialogues with the correct expressions. Then listen and check.**

So do I! × 2   Oh, that reminds me! × 2   I know what you mean, × 2

1 **A:** Tomorrow is our jazz performance at school. I feel nervous.

B: ¹ ___So do I!___ But we've practised a lot, so we'll be fine.

A: That's true, but I always worry about making mistakes.

B: ² _____ but you need to relax. Let's go to the shopping centre.

A: ³ _____ I need to buy a new shirt for the performance!

2 **A:** Are you going to film the student concert this afternoon?

B: Yes, I am. ⁴ _____ I need to charge my camera.

A: I think the concert is going to be great.

B: ⁵ _____ It's always a fun event.

A: The only problem is the old chairs in the hall aren't very comfortable.

B: ⁶ _____ those chairs are so hard!

4 ✳ **Work in pairs. Write another dialogue for each expression. Then act out the dialogues.**

Grammar

verbs + -*ing* form or infinitive

1 🎧(9.9) **Listen and circle the correct answers.**

 Emma   **Mark**   **Sarah**

1 A Emma enjoys playing the … .

   a guitar **b** trumpet **c** (violin)

  B She hopes to win a competition … .

   a next   **b** next   **c** next
     week   month   year

2 A Mark likes having … on his smartphone.

   a podcasts **b** songs **c** films

  B This afternoon he wants to buy … .

   a batteries **b** headphones **c** speakers

3 A Sarah will learn to play … this year.

   a the piano **b** the drums **c** the flute

  B She will also keep practising … .

   a karate **b** basketball **c** gymnastics

2 **Read and complete the sentences with the -*ing* form or the infinitive.**

1 My parents like _____going_____ (go) to jazz festivals in the summer.

2 Lukas promised _____ (call) us as soon as he got home.

3 Let me know when you've finished _____ (read) that book.

4 I always enjoy _____ (see) my friends at the weekend.

5 Isabella is hoping _____ (win) the gymnastics competition.

6 Do you want _____ (come) to my birthday party next Saturday?

7 My best friend loves _____ (write) the school blog. She writes it every week.

8 I hope to learn _____ (speak) Chinese when I go to university.

3 **Read and complete the interview. Use the correct verb forms.**

> enjoy/teach hope/be keep/practise
> learn/play ~~like/listen~~ want/have

Ana: Do you ¹ *like listening* to music?

Ben: Yes, I do! I love music. I ² _____ a DJ when I'm older.

Ana: Would you like to ³ _____ a musical instrument?

Ben: Well, I already play the piano, but not very well!

Ana: You'll have to ⁴ _____ if you want to become a better musician.

Ben: Of course! And I also ⁵ _____ guitar lessons one day.

Ana: Really? I know how to play the guitar and I also ⁶ _____ other people.

Ben: That's great! You can teach me!

4 💡 **Read the questionnaire. Circle your answers.**

1	Do you like listening to pop music?	**Y / N**
2	Do you want to be in a band one day?	**Y / N**
3	Do you enjoy performing in public?	**Y / N**
4	Would you like to learn to sing in another language?	**Y / N**
5	Do you hope to become a famous pop star one day?	**Y / N**
6	Would you keep practising if you were famous?	**Y / N**

5 💬 **In pairs, ask and answer the questions in Activity 4.**

》》 Grammar reference, page 126

1 **After you read** Read the story on Pupil's Book page 116 again. Number the sentences in order.

- [ ] **a** They put up some decorations in the gym for the party.
- [ ] **b** James told Tom that he should put down the cakes.
- [ ] **c** When the music started, Tom started dancing.
- [ ] **d** Tom had a messy accident while he was dancing.
- [ ] **e** Tom collected the cakes and took them to the party.
- [ ] **f** They decided to send out party invitations to everyone.
- [1] **g** The students were preparing for their end-of-year party.
- [ ] **h** They reminded people that it was a fancy dress party.

2 Answer the questions. Write complete sentences.

1 Who said that they should give out party invitations? *Marie said they should give out party invitations.*

2 How did James make the invitations better? _____

3 Why did they need to go to the gym early? _____

4 What happened to Tom after he fell over? _____

3 Read the *Work with words* box. Then complete the table.

Work with words

The negative prefix *un-*

We can add the negative prefix *un-* to some adjectives to make their opposites.

*lucky → **unlucky***

*usual → **unusual***

forgettable	1 _unforgettable_
2 _____	unhealthy
fashionable	3 _____
4 _____	untidy
happy	5 _____
6 _____	unkind
clean	7 _____
8 _____	uninteresting

4 Read and complete the sentences with the negative adjectives from Activity 3.

1 I can't forget that film. It was _____*unforgettable*_____.

2 This comedy is so _____. It's really boring to read.

3 Why is your bedroom so _____? It's a mess!

4 Julia is _____ about the English test. She didn't do well in it.

5 Don't be _____ to your friends. Be nice to them!

6 This old jacket is _____. I need a more modern one.

7 We shouldn't eat too many sweets. They're _____.

8 The water in the river is _____. You shouldn't drink it.

5 Write five or more sentences with the negative adjectives from Activity 4.

1 Look and complete the party activities.

 **1**
 **2**
 **3**
 **4**
 **5**
 **6**

1 _Give out invitations_ to people.

2 _____ before the party.

3 _____ costumes.

4 _____ to the guests.

5 _____ display outside.

6 _____ after the party.

2 🎧9.13 Listen to Jack talking about his party and tick (✓) the activities you hear.

Part 1	
✓ put up decorations	☐ make a playlist
☐ give out invitations	☐ welcome his guests
☐ prepare a special meal	☐ put on fancy dress costumes
Part 2	
☐ serve drinks	☐ open gifts
☐ dance to the music	☐ clear up the mess
☐ watch a firework display	☐ write thank-you messages

verb + object + infinitive

3 🎧9.14 Read and complete the dialogues. Then listen and check.

> her/make ~~him/get~~ me/buy
> me/turn on you/tidy

1 A: Is Paul going to the supermarket?

B: Yes, he is. I asked _him to get_ some cola.

2 A: It's dark in this room. I can't see!

B: Do you want _____ the light?

3 A: Sam, I told _____ your room today

B: I know, but I have to do my homework first

4 A: We're going to need fireworks for the part

B: OK. Remind _____ them tomorrow

5 A: What food is Ana bringing to the party?

B: I asked _____ some sandwiches.

4 Use the ideas below to complete the party checklist.

> serve drinks welcome the guests
> put up decorations give out invitations
> clear up the mess write thank-you messages
> make a playlist prepare a special meal

Before the party

1 ask / my parents
   I asked my parents to put up the decorations.

2 remind / my brother
   _____.

During the party

3 tell / my best friend
   _____

4 ask / my friends
   _____.

After the party

5 want / my grandparents
   _____

6 tell / my sister
   _____.

>> Grammar reference, page 126

1 **After you read** Read the text on Pupil's Book page 118 again. What do the sentences describe? Write.

1 It's the place where they have an underwater music festival.   *Florida*

2 It's a music competition that started in 1996.   _____

3 This is where the flash mob played in Berlin, Germany.   _____

4 It includes songs about ocean plants and animals.   _____

5 It's the prize for winning the Air Guitar World Championships.   _____

6 It's the place where the flash mob danced to Michael Jackson.   _____

2 Read the sentences and circle *T* (true) or *F* (false). Then explain your answers.

1 About 10,000 people were at the Air Guitar World Championships in 1996.   (T)/ F   *No, it was last year.*

2 Air guitar competitors don't know all the songs they will play.   T / F   _____

3 The Underwater Music Festival takes place every four years.   T / F   _____

4 They don't play real instruments in the Underwater Music Festival.   T / F   _____

5 Flash mobs always play music.   T / F   _____

6 There was a big flash mob with 13,597 people in Berlin.   T / F   _____

3 (9.16) Listen to a report about another music festival. Complete the notes.

Electric Forest Festival

Location:	Rothbury, Michigan, [1] _____the USA_____
Year started:	First held in [2] _____
Time of year:	At the end of [3] _____
Length:	Lasts for [4] _____
Setting:	It takes place in a [5] _____
Music styles:	Electronic and [6] _____ music
Audience:	About [7] _____ people
Special features:	Amazing [8] _____ shows at night

4 Work in groups. Choose one of the festivals from the box and find answers to the questions. Write about your festival.

Vive Latino (Mexico)   Strawberry Music Festival (California, USA)
Rock in Rio (Brazil)   Bluesfest (Byron Bay, Australia)

1 Where does the festival take place?

2 When is the festival celebrated?

3 What is the setting of the festival?

4 What type of music can you enjoy?

5 How many people usually go there?

6 What special features are there?

English in action
Saying thank you and responding to thanks

1 (9.19) **Read and complete the dialogue. Then listen and check.**

a Thanks so much	**e** you don't have to do that
b Many thanks for everything	**f** I love organising parties
c Don't mention it	**g** Oh, it's a pleasure
d Many thanks for your help	**h** Thanks a million for making it

Paul: Everything's ready and it looks amazing!

Amy: Yes, it does! The decorations are beautiful.

Paul: ¹ _d Many thanks for your help_ , Amy.

Amy: No worries! ² _____!

Paul: Yes, and you're also very good at it!

Amy: ³ _____!

Paul: The food smells great. ⁴ _____.

Amy: ⁵ _____. Now, I'll prepare some drinks.

Paul: OK. I'm really grateful, but ⁶ _____.

Amy: ⁷ _____. And I'll have something to drink, too!

Paul: Look! People are arriving. ⁸ _____!

Amy: You're welcome. Now go and say hello to your guests!

2 💬 **Work with your partner. Read the situations and take turns saying thank you and responding to thanks.**

1 A friend helped you finish your Art project.

3 You couldn't find your way to the new shopping centre and someone gave you directions.

2 A family member bought you a gift for your birthday.

4 You lost your bag and someone returned it you.

> Thanks so much for helping me finish my Art project!

> Don't mention it.

Pronunciation

3 (9.20) 💬 **Match the two parts of the sentences. Listen and repeat. Remember that we don't stress the *to* part of infinitives. Then practise with a partner.**

1 I hope to become	**a** to play the guitar.
2 I promise to keep	**b** a teacher one day.
3 I could teach you	**c** to hand in your project on time.
4 I asked everyone	**d** my bedroom tidy.
5 I told you to bring	**e** to arrive on time.
6 I reminded you	**f** some party snacks.

Literacy: descriptions

Reading

Words in context

1 Read and complete the sentences.

excitement ~~experience~~ full moon mist powder rainbow

1 There was a lot of ___excitement___ at the concert. Everyone was shouting and waving at the band.

2 When we went camping, we looked into the sky at night and saw the _____.

3 After the storm, we could see a big, beautiful _____ in the sky.

4 What is this coloured _____ on your face? Were you using paints?

5 I enjoyed the air guitar competition. It was an amazing _____!

6 People must be very careful driving when there is _____ in the air.

2 Read the article on Pupil's Book page 120 again. Match the two parts of the sentences.

1 The festival
2 The celebrations
3 The taxi driver
4 The powder
5 The people
6 The writer

a welcomed the writer to the celebrations.
b were dancing and laughing in the street.
c started on the night before the festival.
d hopes to go to the Holi Festival again.
e happens at the start of spring in India.
f looked like a mist or rainbow in the air.

3 Answer the questions. Write complete sentences.

1 In which months does the Holi Festival usually take place?

The Holi Festival usually takes place in February or March.

2 Where did the writer tell stories with friends?

_____

3 What special gift did the taxi driver give to the writer?

_____

4 How did the powder get into the writer's mouth?

_____

5 How did the writer's clothes get wet in the square?

_____

6 How did the writer cool down when it got hot?

_____

4 Work in groups. Choose a special event to celebrate at your school. Discuss the questions and make notes. Then share your ideas with the class.

1 What special event will you celebrate?
2 When will the event take place?
3 What activities will everyone do?

4 What special clothes or costumes will you wear?
5 What decorations will you put up?
6 What will people eat or drink?

Literacy: descriptions

Writing

1 **Read and complete the sentences with 's or s'.**

1 Nora has a cat. _____Nora's_____ cat is black.

2 My parents have a car. My _____ car is new.

3 Berat has two sisters. His _____ room is big.

4 The town has a festival. The _____ festival is in May.

5 The teacher has a desk. The _____ desk is at the front of the class.

6 Those are my friends. My _____ names are Ben and Katerina.

2 **Choose an exciting festival you know. Then plan a description for an online article.**

Explain what the festival is about. → _____

Say when and where it takes place. → _____

Describe what people see and do. → _____

Describe what people hear or listen to. → _____

Describe what people smell and taste. → _____

Use *like* to make comparisons. → _____

Say why you like this festival and why people should go to it. → _____

3 **Now write your description.**

4 **Check your work. Tick (✓) the steps when you have done them.**

Have I used interesting adjectives? ☐

Have I included different senses? ☐

Have I used apostrophes correctly? ☐

Have I used *-ing* forms and infinitives correctly? ☐

1   **Unscramble the letters. Then write the words.**

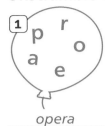     

1	2	3	4	5	6
p r o a e	n o i i v l	b r e y k a d o	a o c u k r s n t d	e t r m u o t p	a o h r r s c e t

<u>opera</u>   _____   _____   _____   _____   _____

2   **Read and complete the sentences.**

decorations   firework   ~~guests~~   invitations   mess   playlist

1   You should go to the door and welcome your _____*guests*_____ .

2   The party was fun, but now we have to clear up the _____ .

3   Thank you so much for making a _____ of songs for the party.

4   On New Year's Eve, my family and I usually watch a _____ display.

5   Let's put up some _____ for your party. They'll look really good.

6   Jack didn't give out _____ . He sent email messages.

3   **Read the sentences. Are they correct (✓) or incorrect (✗)? Rewrite the incorrect sentences.**

1   I'm going to keep to study until 9 pm.   [✗]   *I'm going to keep studying until 9 pm.*

2   Do you enjoy going to festivals?   [ ]   _____

3   My sister hopes becoming an opera singer.   [ ]   _____

4   I really want to visit India one day.   [ ]   _____

5   Sam promised sending me a postcard.   [ ]   _____

4   **Rewrite the sentences using the verb in brackets.**

1   Cecilia showed me how to dance. (teach)   *Cecilia taught me to dance.*

2   Dad said that we should tidy up. (want)   _____

3   Rennie told Henry, 'Be on time.' (remind)   _____

4   Mum said to me, 'Go to bed.' (tell)   _____

5   We said, 'Please can you wait, Lisa.' (ask)   _____

Self-evaluation

5   **Answer the questions about your work in Unit 9.**

1   How was your work in this unit? Choose.   [ ] OK   [ ] Good   [ ] Excellent

2   Which lesson was your favourite? _____

3   Which parts of the unit were difficult for you? _____

4   What new things can you talk about now? _____

5   How can you work and learn better next year? _____

Get ready for...

B1 Preliminary for Schools Listening Part 4

 1 Read the task carefully. Make sure you know what you have to do.

 2  Listen and choose the correct answer. Then explain your answer.

What time will Derek go to Helen's studio?

A About four o'clock

B After five o'clock

C Before he practises for his concert

_____

_____

_____

Do! **3** 🎯 (9.23) **For each question, choose the correct answer. You will hear an interview with a musician named Derek.**

1 Derek has just finished ...

  A performing on his new tour.

  B recording a new album.

  C performing with an orchestra.

> **tip Exam**
>
> First, read and listen to the instructions. Then, use the pauses to read the questions and think about the context. This may be information about places and events or people's lives, interests and experiences.

2 How long ago was Derek on the show?

  A twelve years ago

  B thirteen years ago

  C thirty years ago

3 For his newest album ...

  A Derek sang with an orchestra.

  B Derek played the drums on all the songs.

  C Derek wrote the music for ten new songs.

4 Derek's show will be different this year because ...

  A there will be costumes and fireworks.

  B it starts next month.

  C there won't be a live orchestra.

5 People can buy tickets ...

  A online.

  B right now at ticket offices.

  C at half past ten this evening.

B1 Preliminary for Schools Reading Part 6

Think! **1** **Read the task carefully. Make sure you know what you have to do.**

Try! **2** **Read and complete the sentences. Use only one word in each gap.**

1 Many families put up decorations in their homes _____*at*_____ Christmas time.

2 Have you ever wanted _____ be a professional musician and play in an orchestra?

3 I'd recommend _____ you give out invitations tomorrow, if you want your friends to come to your party.

Do! **3** 🎯 **Read the text below and think of the word which best fits each gap. Use only one word in each gap. There is an example at the beginning.**

tip **Exam**

Look at the example at the beginning of the text before you start and identify why it is correct.

Spring Sound

I think Spring Sound is one of the **(1)** _____*best*_____ folk music festivals that I've ever been to. I really love it. I went there last spring with a friend and we had an amazing time. I'm planning **(2)** _____ go there again this year, but this time with a larger group of friends.

The festival always takes place during the last weekend **(3)** _____ April on an old farm about two kilometres outside the town **(4)** _____ I live. Last year, more **(5)** _____ twenty different bands and singers performed and the total audience was about ten thousand people. That's fantastic for a local festival.

If you decide to go to Spring Sound this year, remember to wear boots and bring a raincoat. The **(6)** _____ can be wet in April. You might also want to bring food, although you can buy burgers and other fast food there. You can **(7)** _____ buy T-shirts and other souvenirs. See you there!

Language booster 3

1 After you read **Read the text on Pupil's Book page 124 again. Answer the questions.**

1 Who plays the keyboard in Tessa's band? _Tessa_

2 Who plays the trumpet? _____

3 Who plays the violin? _____

4 Who started the band? _____

5 Who will announce the winner of the competition? _____

6 Who will serve the drinks at the party? _____

2 Read and write the music words. What's the mystery word?

1 when you entertain an audience by singing, dancing or acting

2 a metal musical instrument that you blow

3 a wooden musical instrument with four strings and a long stick

4 a style of music that was first played in the USA around 1900

5 an electronic musical instrument similar to a piano

6 a musical instrument that you hit with sticks or your hands

1	P	E	R	F	O	R	M	A	N	C	E
2	T										
3	V										
4	J										
5	K										
6	D										

The mystery word is _____.

3 Read and match the sentence halves.

1 The orchestra played

2 We took part

3 The children danced

4 My parents served

5 Mr Jenks announced

6 Sarah won

a drinks at the party.

b a prize in the competition!

c the winner of the race.

d in a competition at school.

e to the music all evening.

f a tune at the concert.

4 Answer the questions.

1 What's your favourite musical instrument? Why? _____

_____

2 What's your favourite type of music? Why? _____

_____

5 🎧 **Read and listen to the dialogue on Pupil's Book page 125 again. Write True or False.**

1 Josh is eating a lot of cake at the party.   _True_

2 Tessa is surprised that they won the prize at the Band Competition.   _____

3 Josh leaves the party before Tessa.   _____

4 Tessa's mum is picking her up from the party.   _____

5 Josh and Tessa aren't going to practise tomorrow morning.   _____

6 Josh and Tessa are going to take part in more competitions.   _____

6 **Complete the dialogue with the words below.**

~~go~~   Bye   See   soon   you

Mario: It's been a great game, but I've got to **(1)** _____go_____ .

Leah: Oh, no. Don't go yet!

Mario: Sorry! My dad's waiting for me. See **(2)** _____ later.

Leah: Yes, see you **(3)** _____ .

Mario: Yes, very soon! **(4)** _____ you tomorrow at the party!

Leah: Of course! **(5)** _____ .

7 ✳ **Write another dialogue using expressions for saying goodbye. Use the dialogue in Activity 6 to help you.**

_____

_____

_____

_____

_____

_____

8 💡 **Look back at the Pupil's Book and answer the questions.**

1 What was your favourite unit? Why?

_____

2 Who was your favourite character? Why?

_____

3 What was your favourite text? Why?

_____

Grammar reference

1

Lesson 3: *used to*

1 **Read and complete.**

used to			
I / You / He / She / It / We / They	1 _____used to_____ ✓	be noisy. play games.	
	2 _____ ✗		
Did	I / you / he / she / it / we / they	3 _____	be noisy? play games?
Yes,	I / you / he / she / it / we / they	4 _____ ✓	
No,		5 _____ ✗	

did
didn't
didn't use to
use to
~~used to~~

2 **Write sentences with *used to*.**

1 I / watch / cartoons ✓   *I used to watch cartoons.*
2 They / play / in the park ✓   _____
3 Ben / eat / ice cream ✓   _____
4 We / go / camping ✗   _____
5 Mel and Kim / tidy up ✗   _____
6 You / wear / jeans ✓   _____

Lesson 5: Present continuous and Present simple for future

3 **Read and complete.**

Present continuous and Present simple for future
We use the ¹ _____Present continuous_____ to talk about arrangements for the future, e.g. we can talk about our personal ² _____ for the weekend.
We use the ³ _____ to talk about ⁴ _____ , e.g. we can talk about when things happen.

Present simple
plans
~~Present continuous~~
timetables

4 **Read and complete the sentences with the correct present tenses.**

1 My grandparents _____aren't coming_____ (not/come) to visit. They're too busy.
2 The film _____ (start) at seven o'clock. I checked the time online.
3 I _____ (meet) Julie after school today to study for the test.
4 The bank _____ (not/open) tomorrow. It's Saturday.
5 The next train _____ (leave) from platform 2.
6 We _____ (not/have) supper now. It's only 3 pm.

Lesson 3: *will* for predictions

1 **Read and complete.**

won't ~~will~~ will will

will for predictions				
I / You / He / She / It / We / They		1 ___*will*___ ✓	become famous.	
		2 _____ ✗	go to university.	
3 _____	I / you / he / she / it / we / they		go backpacking in Europe?	
When	4 _____	I / you / he / she / It / we / they		get married?

2 **Write questions about the future. Then write true answers for you.**

1 what / you / do / leave school?

   What will you do when you leave school?   I'll... _____

2 what / you / study / at university?

   _____   _____

3 where / you / live / in 2030?

   _____   _____

4 when / you / get married?

   _____   _____

5 when / you / retire?

   _____   _____

Lesson 5: *might, may* and *could* for predictions

3 **Read and tick (✓) the sentences you agree with.**

might, may and *could* for predictions
☐ **1** I **might** get married before I'm thirty.
☐ **2** I **may** retire before I'm sixty.
☐ **3** I **could** get a degree one day.
☐ **4** I **might** not go to university.
☐ **5** I **may** not have children.

4 **Read and complete the sentences with predictions about the future.**

1 People might *speak only one language in the future* .

2 I may study _____.

3 My family could _____.

4 I might not learn _____.

5 I may not want to _____.

Lesson 3: Reported speech: statements

1 **Read and complete.**

| their | ~~he~~ | her | they |

| ~~didn't like~~ | enjoyed | wanted | were |

Reported speech: statements
Berat told me, 'I don't like mystery stories.' Berat told me that [1]_____ *he* _____ [2]_____ *didn't like* _____ mystery stories.
My friends said, 'We are interested in graphic novels.' My friends said that [3]_____ [4]_____ interested in graphic novels.
Carlotta said, 'My parents want to visit England.' Carlotta said that [5]_____ parents [6]_____ to visit England.
The children told us, 'We enjoy riding our bikes.' The children told us that they [7]_____ riding [8]_____ bikes.

2 **Rewrite the sentences as reported speech.**

1 me → my mother: 'I don't feel well.'   *I told my mother that I didn't feel well.*

2 the boys: 'We have to go home.'   _____

3 Sam → me: 'You're my best friend.'   _____

4 us: 'We don't like cold weather.'   _____

5 Lucia → Ted: 'You're really funny!'   _____

Lesson 5: Present simple and Past simple passive

3 **Read and complete.**

Present simple and Past simple passive	
They used stone to **make** the castle. The castle [1]_____ *is made* _____ of stone.	Many visitors **take** photos of the castle. Photos of the castle [2]_____ by many visitors.
They **damaged** the castle during the war. The castle [3]_____ during the war.	They **fixed** all the problems ten years ago. All the problems [4]_____ ten years ago.

4 **Read and complete the sentences with the Present or Past simple passive.**

1 There used to be a famous painting over there, but it _____ *was stolen* _____ (steal) a long time ago.

2 Thousands of graphic novels _____ (buy) by young people every month.

3 The Eiffel Tower _____ (visit) by millions of tourists every year.

4 In ancient times, most buildings _____ (make) of wood and stone.

5 The Hagia Sofia in Istanbul _____ (build) hundreds of years ago.

Lesson 3: Modal verbs of obligation

1 **Read and complete.**

Modal verbs of obligation		
We	¹ _should_ must ² _____	try to save water. ³ _____ plastic. plant more trees.
We	shouldn't ⁴ _____	waste water. throw away plastic. ⁵ _____ our forests.
We	needn't	⁶ _____ a lot of water. buy another magazine.

mustn't
destroy
need to
recycle
use
~~should~~

2 **Write the sentences with the correct modal verbs.**

1 We shouldn't recycle plastic.   _We should recycle plastic._

2 People must waste water.   _____

3 You needn't eat fruit every day.   _____

4 I need to go everywhere by car.   _____

5 We should destroy the rainforests.   _____

6 He mustn't pick up rubbish in the park.   _____

Lesson 5: Reported speech: questions and commands

3 **Read and complete.**

Reported speech: *Wh-* questions
Sam asked us, 'Where ¹ _is_ the swimming pool?'   Sam asked us where the swimming pool ² _____ .

Reported speech: *yes/no* questions
I asked Amy, 'Does your family ³ _____ a lot of plastic?'   I asked Amy ⁴ _____ her family ⁵ _____ a lot of plastic.

Reported speech: commands
Dad told me, 'Be careful and ⁶ _____ start any fires'.   Dad told me to ⁷ _____ careful and ⁸ _____ to start any fires.

be
don't
if
~~is~~
not
recycle
recycled
was

4 **Write the questions and commands as reported speech.**

1 Mum asked me, 'Do you want a biscuit?'   _Mum asked me if I wanted a biscuit._

2 Tom told us, 'Don't make any noise.'   _____

3 Lisa asked Dan, 'Are you feeling OK?'   _____

4 I asked Tom, 'When do you study?'   _____

5 Kate told Zoe, 'Turn off the TV.'   _____

6 I asked Ana, 'Where's my book?'   _____

5 Grammar reference

Lesson 3: Reflexive pronouns

1 **Read and complete.**

> ourselves   themselves   yourself   herself   ~~myself~~   itself

Reflexive pronouns			
I can see [1] _myself_		We can see [5] _____ .	
You can see [2] _____		You can see yourselves	in the mirror.
He can see himself	in the mirror.	They can see [6] _____	
She can see [3] _____			
It can see [4] _____			

2 **Complete the questions. Then write the answers for you.**

1 Have you ever hurt _____ _yourself_ _____ while doing a sport?   _____

2 Does your friend ever talk to _____ in class?   _____

3 Should we take care of _____ by eating healthy food?   _____

4 Does your tablet turn _____ off if you aren't using it?   _____

5 Do you ever think, 'I'm proud of _____?'   _____

Lesson 5: Past perfect

3 **Read and complete.**

> had finished   had seen   hadn't planned   ~~hadn't walked~~

Past perfect
I [1] _hadn't walked_ very far before I saw the bay.
After we [2] _____ our homework, we watched TV.
She [3] _____ the penguin dive into the water before it caught a fish.
They [4] _____ their holiday very well, so it wasn't fun.

4 **Read and complete the sentences with the Past simple and the Past perfect.**

1 I _____ _went_ _____ (go) for a run after I _____ _had put on_ _____ (put on) my trainers.

2 Sam _____ (be) friends with Bob for a year before I _____ (meet) him.

3 After we _____ (finish) lunch, we _____ (do) the washing up.

4 Isidora _____ (visit) the USA many times before she _____ (go) to New York.

5 Before my parents _____ (arrive) home, I _____ (tidy) my bedroom.

Lesson 3: Zero and first conditionals

1 **Read and circle.**

Zero conditional
1 If I (need) / will need new clothes, my parents give me money.
2 If you had / have a problem, you should ask me for help.
3 What do / did you do if you don't like something you have bought?

First conditional
4 If I save enough money, I'll buy / I buy a new phone.
5 If that happens / will happen, we'll be very disappointed.
6 What will Katerina do if she can't / couldn't find her bag?

2 **Write sentences with the zero (Z) or first (F) conditional.**

1 I / arrive / late / I / feel bad (Z)   *If I arrive late, I feel bad.*

2 we / help / Ann / she / be / happy (F)   _____

3 you / be / busy / we / can / talk / later (Z)   _____

4 an accident / happen / I / call / you (F)   _____

5 What / you / eat / you / want / a snack (Z)   _____

Lesson 5: Second conditional

3 **Read and complete.**

could   ~~had~~   won   were

Second conditional
1 I I _____*had*_____ only one wish, I'd ask for a long and happy life.
2 If I _____ be invisible, I'd help the police catch criminals.
3 If you _____ the leader of your country, what would you do?
4 If you _____ 100 pounds in the lottery, what would you buy?

4 **Write sentences about you and people you know. Use your own ideas.**

1 If I _____*could*_____ (can) travel into space, I _____*would visit*_____ (visit) Mars.

2 If you _____ (know) a big secret, _____ (you / tell) me?

3 If people _____ (take) care of our planet, it _____ (be) a nicer place to live.

4 If you _____ (meet) a famous actor, _____ (you / feel) nervous?

5 If I _____ (have) a party, I _____ (invite) everyone that I know.

Lesson 3: *(not) as ... as*

1 Read and complete.

big cold dangerous exciting good nervous ~~tall~~ well

as ... as
I'm as ¹_____tall_____ as my sister, but she's two years older than me.
You're as ²_____ at sports as Tom. How much do you practice?
We dance as ³_____ as they do, but we also dance more often.
Today is as ⁴_____ as it was yesterday. It's only about 10ºC outside.

not as ... as
Tennis can be boring. It isn't as ⁵_____ as football.
I'm not as ⁶_____ speaking in public as you. I'm more relaxed.
Liverpool isn't as ⁷_____ as London. Liverpool is smaller.
Dogs aren't as ⁸_____ as wild animals.

2 Compare yourself with people you know. Write sentences with *(not) as ... as*.

1 tall   *I'm (not) as tall as my sister.*   4 keen on sports   _____

2 confident   _____   5 bad at singing   _____

3 good at Maths _____   6 nervous before a test _____

Lesson 5: Question tags

3 Read and complete.

are we does she do they aren't you has she haven't they ~~is it~~ isn't he

Question tags	
Today isn't Monday, ¹_____*is it*_____?	Your parents don't travel, ⁵_____?
Adam's very friendly, ²_____?	Kim doesn't like pop music, ⁶_____?
We aren't late for our English lesson, ³_____?	Your friends have left, ⁷_____?
You're going out, ⁴_____?	Nina hasn't arrived yet, ⁸_____?

4 Write tag questions.

1 Tom plays football, _____*doesn't he*_____?   5 Miguel's quite clever, _____?

2 Tomorrow isn't a holiday, _____?   6 Your friends haven't phoned, _____?

3 Lucy has gone home, _____?   7 We're in the same Art class, _____?

4 The bus doesn't stop here, _____?   8 You don't like eating fish, _____?

Lesson 3: Relative pronouns

1 **Read and complete.**

> that   when   where   which   ~~who~~   whose

Relative pronouns
Florence Nightingale was a woman [1]_____*who*_____ started the first nursing school.
Penicillin is an antibiotic [2]_____ / [3]_____ is used all around the world.
Stockholm is the city [4]_____ the Nobel Prize is awarded every year.
I remember the time [5]_____ you and I visited the Science Museum in London.
Alexander Fleming was a scientist [6]_____ invention has saved many lives.

2 **Circle the correct relative pronouns.**

1 I like people (whose) / **that** / **who** interests are similar to mine.

2 Summer is the time **where** / **when** / **which** most families take holidays.

3 Have you ever invented something **when** / **that** / **whose** was useful?

4 I need to find someone **which** / **who** / **where** can teach me to play the piano.

5 Buenos Aires is a city **where** / **when** / **that** you can visit lots of museums.

6 This is the tablet **when** / **whose** / **which** I got from my parents for my birthday.

Lesson 5: Embedded questions

3 **Read and complete.**

> I wonder   ~~can you~~   you know   you tell

Embedded questions	
Where are we going?	[1]_____*Can you*_____ tell us where we are going?
When does the film start?	Could [2]_____ me when the film starts?
Is this my medicine?	Do [3]_____ if / whether this is my medicine?
Are these pills safe?	[4]_____ if / whether these pills are safe?

4 **Imagine you're at a museum. Ask questions at the information desk.**

1 Can you tell me _____

2 I wonder if _____

3 Could you tell me _____

4 Do you know whether _____

9 Grammar reference

Lesson 3: Verb patterns: -ing / infinitive

1 Read and complete.

verb + *-ing* form
I liked [1] _____*decorating*_____ the room for the party. It was fun!
Cristina keeps [2] _____ the guitar every day after school.
We finished [3] _____ up the mess, but it took an hour.

verb + infinitive
You hope [4] _____ good marks in your final exam.
Sam is learning [5] _____ Italian food.
My parents promise [6] _____ me a new bike this year.

clearing
~~decorating~~
practising
to buy
to get
to make

2 Complete the sentences with the *-ing* form or the infinitive.

1 When will you finish _____*preparing*_____ (prepare) food for the party?

2 I promise _____ (work) on my Science project today.

3 One day, I'll learn _____ (speak) French or German.

4 Sam hopes _____ (study) medicine in future.

5 I keep _____ (make) mistakes because I'm not careful.

Lesson 5: Verb patterns: object + infinitive

3 Read and complete.

verb + object + infinitive
I wanted you [1] _____*to give*_____ out the party invitations.
Ana told Paul [2] _____ a fancy dress costume.
Zeynep taught us [3] _____ a playlist on the computer.
We asked the children [4] _____ quiet during the film.
You reminded me [5] _____ Amanda this morning.

to be
to call
~~to give~~
to make
to wear

4 Order the words and write the sentences.

1 asked | friend | help | serve | me | drinks | the | to | my
   My friend asked me to help serve the drinks.

2 you | invitations | me | out | give | do | want | to | the | ?
   _____

3 everyone | clear | mess | I | told | not | up | to | the
   _____

4 you | make | me | can | remind | a | to | playlist | ?
   _____

5 teacher | us | play | keyboard | the | our | taught | to
   _____

Wordlist

Unit 1

City tourism

accommodation _____

backpacker _____

capital city _____

clock tower _____

fountain _____

luggage _____

monument _____

police station _____

statue _____

tour guide _____

tourist _____

tourist information centre _____

Travel and transport

coach _____

crossroads _____

fire engine _____

lorry _____

neighbourhood _____

pavement _____

railway station _____

road sign _____

roundabout _____

taxi _____

traffic jam _____

traffic lights _____

Unit 2

Jobs

architect _____

computer programmer _____

dentist _____

diver _____

graphic designer _____

hairdresser _____

inventor _____

journalist _____

manager _____

novelist _____

politician _____

professional footballer _____

Life events

be born _____

grow up _____

go to school _____

go to university _____

get a degree _____

go backpacking _____

find a job _____

fall in love _____

get married _____

have children _____

move house _____

retire _____

W Wordlist

Unit 3

Books

adventure story _____

biography _____

detective story _____

drama _____

fantasy _____

graphic novel _____

horror story _____

mystery story _____

poetry _____

recipe book _____

romance _____

science fiction _____

Adjectives to describe places

bright _____

charming _____

dark _____

empty _____

gorgeous _____

huge _____

popular _____

secret _____

steep _____

strange _____

terrible _____

tiny _____

Unit 4

The environment

climate change _____

destroy the rainforests _____

global warming _____

pick up rubbish _____

plant trees _____

pollution _____

protect the environment _____

recycle _____

save water _____

switch off lights _____

use renewable energy _____

waste energy _____

Extreme weather

avalanche _____

drought _____

flood _____

forest fire _____

gale _____

heatwave _____

hurricane _____

lightning _____

snowstorm _____

thunder _____

tornado _____

tsunami _____

volcano _____

Unit 5

Extreme sports

diving   _____

go-karting   _____

golf   _____

horse-riding   _____

ice hockey   _____

jogging   _____

kite surfing   _____

motor-racing   _____

rock climbing   _____

squash   _____

surfboarding   _____

water skiing   _____

Geography

bay   _____

field   _____

scenery   _____

sunrise   _____

sunset   _____

tide   _____

valley   _____

wood (= forest)   _____

north   _____

south   _____

east   _____

west   _____

Unit 6

Shopping

credit card   _____

customer   _____

designer labels   _____

exchange (v)   _____

get a refund   _____

on sale   _____

online shopping   _____

queue   _____

receipt   _____

second-hand   _____

shop assistant   _____

till   _____

Imaginary situations

be invisible   _____

become a book
   or film character _____

become the leader
   of your country   _____

donate to a charity _____

go into space   _____

have a lot of money _____

have three wishes _____

meet a famous person _____

pass exams   _____

travel back in time _____

travel the world   _____

win a cup   _____

Unit 7

Communication

chat to friends _____

get on well _____

have an argument _____

insert an emoji _____

keep a promise _____

keep a secret _____

listen to a podcast _____

receive a text message _____

tell a lie _____

tell the truth _____

use social media _____

watch a vlog _____

Feelings

calm _____

confused _____

curious _____

delighted _____

disappointed _____

embarrassed _____

jealous _____

miserable _____

nervous _____

proud _____

serious _____

upset _____

Unit 8

Inventions

aeroplane _____

antibiotics _____

battery _____

electricity _____

light bulb _____

photography _____

radio _____

spacecraft _____

steam engine _____

vaccination _____

wheel _____

X-ray _____

Health and medicine

feel better _____

feel ill _____

get a prescription _____

have a fever _____

have an injection _____

have an operation _____

have an X-ray _____

take some pills _____

carry out an experiment _____

do some research _____

make a discovery _____

win a prize _____

Unit 9

Music

drums	_____
flute	_____
folk music	_____
jazz music	_____
keyboard	_____
opera	_____
orchestra	_____
performance	_____
rock music	_____
soundtrack	_____
trumpet	_____
violin	_____

Having a party

clear up the mess	_____
dance to the music	_____
give out invitations	_____
make a playlist	_____
open your gifts	_____
prepare a special meal	_____
put on fancy dress costumes	_____
put up decorations	_____
serve drinks	_____
watch a firework display	_____
welcome your guests	_____
write thank-you messages	_____

Irregular verbs

Cover the Past simple and Past participle columns and check what you remember!

Infinitive	Past simple		Past participle	
be	was/were		been	
break	broke		broken	
bring	brought		brought	
buy	bought		bought	
catch	caught		caught	
choose	chose		chosen	
come	came		come	
cost	cost		cost	
cut	cut		cut	
do	did		done	
draw	drew		drawn	
drink	drank		drunk	
drive	drove		driven	
eat	ate		eaten	
fall	fell		fallen	
feel	felt		felt	
find	found		found	
fly	flew		flown	
get	got		got	
give	gave		given	
go	went		gone/been	
have	had		had	
hear	heard		heard	
hit	hit		hit	
hold	held		held	
keep	kept		kept	
know	knew		known	

Infinitive	Past simple		Past participle	
learn	learned		learned	
leave	left		left	
let	let		let	
lose	lost		lost	
make	made		made	
meet	met		met	
pay	paid		paid	
put	put		put	
read	read		read	
ride	rode		ridden	
run	ran		run	
say	said		said	
see	saw		seen	
sell	sold		sold	
send	sent		sent	
sing	sang		sung	
sleep	slept		slept	
stand	stood		stood	
take	took		taken	
teach	taught		taught	
tell	told		told	
think	thought		thought	
throw	threw		thrown	
wake	woke		woken	
wear	wore		worn	
win	won		won	
write	wrote		written	

Progress path

Read and write. Then tick.

Add labels.

1

_____

2

_____

Starter Unit

What's your favourite hobby? _____

Why? _____

Unit 1

When I was three,
I used to _____.
I didn't use to

_____.

Unit 4

Write two things we <u>should</u> do and two things we <u>shouldn't</u> do to help the environment.

✔ _____

✔ _____

✗ _____

✗ _____

Unit 2

Add labels.

1

_____

2

_____

Unit 3

Hi, my name is Sophie. I love detective stories.

She said that her name _____.
She said _____.

Unit 6

1 If I want some new clothes, I _____.

2 If I don't have any cash, I _____.

Unit 7

Add question tags.

1 You're embarrassed, _____?

2 This isn't a very good vlog, _____?

Unit 8

Add labels.

1

It gives us light and heat.

_____

2

It saves a lot of lives.

_____

Unit 9

1 I enjoy **to play** / **playing** basketball.

2 We hope **to go** / **going** to the beach on Saturday.

Pearson Education Limited
KAO Two
KAO Park
Hockham Way,
Harlow, Essex,
CM17 9SR England
and Associated Companies throughout the world.

www.english.com/teamtogether

The publishers would like to thank Anna Osborn for her contribution.

First published 2020
Fourth impression 2025

ISBN: 978-1-292-29262-5

Set in Fruitger Neue LT 11pt

Printed in Slovakia by Neografia

Acknowledgements:
The publishers would like to thank teachers from schools in Madrid, Spain,
Istanbul, Turkey and Ankara, Turkey for their feedback and comments during the
development of the materials.

Image Credit(s):

123RF.com: Deklofenak 134, Derek Audette 4, dglimages 82,
domenicogelermo 4, 8, Ekarin Apirakthanakorn 4, georgerudy 34, Jovan
Mandic 85, Kasto 61, Ienanet 18, Natalia Sheinkin 9, Nicolasmenijes 80, Oleksii
Hrecheniuk 71, Pongsakorn Tantiyakorn 17, ronniechua 8, Ruslan Huzau 20,
stockbroker 96, Tatiana Popova 4, 9, Wavebreak Media Ltd 67, yuriz 81; **Alamy
Stock Photo:** Hero Images Inc 135, Idris Ahmed 111, Juice Images 23, Keren
Su 71, Oote Boe 1 99, Porntep Lueangon 77, Raga Jose Fuste 71, Ralph Lee
Hopkins 47, Vdbvsl 11; **Getty Images:** Andersen Ross 110, GlobalStock 116,
Kevin Dodge 98, marcduf 64, mixetto 79, Steve Debenport 38, Westend61
61; **Pearson Education Asia Ltd:** Cheuk-king Lo 93; **Pearson Education
Ltd:** Antonio Marcos Díaz 2, 3, 5, 17, 29, 40, 43, 67, 78, 81, 93, 105, 116,
Gareth Boden 60, Jules Selmes 18, 82, 96, 106, Justin Hoffmann 96, Studio 8
106; **Shutterstock.com:** 1980302 97, Alexandre Zveiger 105, Andy Dean
Photography 106, Basyn 16, Bill45 61, Butterfly Hunter 47, Claudia Veja
Images 16, Dardalnna 134, DennisvandenElzen 47, Edhar 40, Elya Vatel 134,
ESB Professional 114, Fedor Selivanov 85, FocusStocker 68, Fotokon 78,
GaudiLab 16, Halina Yakushevich 72, Haveseen 135, IVASHstudio 21, JiroTX
21, Jorg Hackemann 59, Juliya Shangarey 87, Kadek Bonit Permadi 47, Mandy
Godbehear 86, Marcin Balcerzak 134, Marcus Bay 16, Marian Fil 4, Marzolino 94,
melis 109, Milanzeremski 16, Netfalls - Remy Musser 64, noche 25, ocphoto 33,
Oleksandr_Delyk 101, Olena Yakobchuk 16, Pingebat 85, Rapaeh 21, Shchipkova
Elena 61, Sira Anamwong 51, Stephen Bonk 64, Tetra Images 96, Tony
Magdaraog 21, Vera Petrunina 40

Illustrated by José Rubio, Juan Fender, Miguel Calero, Oscar Herrero, Pablo
Torrecilla, Paul McCaffrey, Pep Brocal, Tatio Viana, Christos Skaltsas (Hyphen)
and Zacharias Papadopoulos (Hyphen)

Cover Image: Antonio Marcos Díaz